Via Chicago

Social Fictions Series

Series Editor

Patricia Leavy (*USA*)

International Editorial Advisory Board

VOLUME 33

Via Chicago

By

J. E. Sumerau

BRILL

SENSE

LEIDEN | BOSTON

All chapters in this book have undergone peer review.

The Library of Congress Cataloging-in-Publication Data is available online at http://catalog.loc.gov

ISSN 2542-8799
ISBN 978-90-04-43294-9 (paperback)
ISBN 978-90-04-43295-6 (hardback)
ISBN 978-90-04-43296-3 (e-book)

ADVANCE PRAISE FOR
VIA CHICAGO

"In *Via Chicago*, Sumerau develops explores a nuanced and compelling theme by studying the various ways people impacted by trauma build families of choice. The novel weaves together a series of interconnected narratives in which each character recounts a shared story from their own perspective after reflecting on their own prior traumatic experiences. The characters' past experiences frame readers' understanding of how each character interprets and responds within their current relationships. Sumerau beautifully captures the complexity of hurt people and how our past experiences, whether realized or not, shape how we understand the world. This timely novel is needed more than ever in college classrooms as many young adults, in the light of public conversation on power and abuse, are starting to examine their own traumatic experiences, families, romantic relationships, and importance of place. *Via Chicago* would make a great addition to undergraduate courses addressing sexualities, gender identities, families, geography, LGBTQIA studies, or trauma recovery."
– M. N. Barringer, Ph.D., Assistant Professor, University of North Florida

"'Autonomy, egalitarianisms, and never settle' – these are Ella's 3 rules about non monogamy. While curious, Mercury has experienced too much violence and abuse to believe someone like Ella could love them. Sumerau brings the relationship of Ella and Mercury to her reader as they attempt to negotiate who is allowed to be a part of a family – one that is polyamorous but not a proscribed polyamory based on sexual encounters. Instead Sumerau has us wrapped up in this 'chosen' family's deep interest in friendships and intimate partnerships. Dear Reader – you will want to be part of this family before the end of this novel! The characters are real with a capital 'R.' Sumerau's use of iconic landmarks and local color that mark Chicago, Miami, and Atlanta allows the reader to imagine themselves as part of this family.

For readers who are unfamiliar with polyamory, non monogamy, and intimate friendships this is a primer to imagining and even inspiring chosen family."

– Andrea Miller, Ph.D., Full Adjunct Professor & Fellow at the Institute for Human Rights and Humanitarian Studies, Webster University

"As someone who has both read and used Sumerau's previous novels as teaching tools, I could not be more excited for the release of *Via Chicago. Via Chicago* is a triumphant story about the process of personal growth, family, and healing. Sumerau once again creates vivid characters whose lives speak to relatable themes of love, loss, and the power of support from those closest to you. Through her compelling narrative, Sumerau challenges her readers to recognize the deep and imperfect bonds that emerge through chosen family, and how none of us ever flourish completely alone. Set in the bustling city of Chicago, she seamlessly weaves details of the city into the narrative to construct a rich portrait of the lovable and complicated cast of characters in a context that matches their continual shifts and changes as people. *Via Chicago* will be a favorite for anyone who loves family dramas, LGBTQ focused narratives, and deep character development. Furthermore, this novel will be an indispensable tool for those teaching courses on the family, LGBTQ Studies, social psychology, and more. Read this book; you won't regret it or forget it."

– Lain A. B. Mathers, Ph.D., Assistant Professor, Indiana State University

"In *Via Chicago*, Sumerau offers storytelling for the public good. Her approach to the reader is as if we are a welcomed guest or an insider to the 'interlocking narratives' of characters who become a chosen family. Despite each member's own challenges, they become the life-rafts for each other providing each other enough of what is familiar and what is new as their chosen family becomes the main foundation for companionship, safety, trust, intimacy, mentorship, friendship, and love. I especially recommend this work for learning about families (particularly families of choice and non-monogamous families), LGBTQ people and relationships, place, trauma, and social support. For those seeking or simply interested in learning about families of choice, this book may provide some company and hope. For anyone yearning to help, better understand, or support someone they love, this book may provide insights not found elsewhere. For teachers, administrators, health practitioners, and counselors, this book may open new and improve existing avenues in research, teaching, counseling, treatment, and care."

– **Brittany M. Harder, Ph.D., Assistant Professor, University of Tampa**

Previous Novels by J. E. Sumerau

Cigarettes & Wine

Essence

Homecoming Queens

That Year

Other People's Oysters
(with Alexandra C. H. Nowakowski)

Palmetto Rose

To Eve for teaching me about Samantha Yale and so much more

CONTENTS

CONTENTS

PREFACE

What is a family? How do families develop?

These questions permeate *Via Chicago* as ten people come together as a familial unit after each experiencing and (at least) beginning to recover from prior traumatic experiences. Ella and Linsk are a nonmonogamous couple who have helped one another heal and built an unconventional family together with Case, Kaisa, Reeves, Jo, Andrei, and Michelle over the course of a decade. As the novel begins, Mercury has just moved to Chicago to pursue graduate study when they begin a romantic relationship with Ella and a broader emotional engagement with the family. At the same time, Mercury is beginning to work through traumatic past experiences while Jo might have found love in the form of a new guy the family just calls Twitter Boy. As the novel progresses, we follow Mercury, Jo, and the rest of the family as each relates to their own and others' traumatic experiences and bonds together over these and other shared aspects of their lives, desires, and goals.

Told as a series of interlocking narratives, the novel explores different pathways for managing traumatic experiences as well as the ways people build families of choice in adulthood. As the characters' current and past experiences unfold, each seeks to reconcile both traumatic past experiences that shaped parts of who they are now, and the development of a family, home, and sense of belonging with the others and within the city of Chicago. *Via Chicago* is a novel about the ways families and love can form out of shared experiences, connections, and traumas as well as the ways our past influences our current and future selves. Built via the interconnecting narratives of multiple characters who are at different points both within the family and in their own healing, *Via Chicago* shows us how social support and a sense of belonging can develop out of and facilitate recovery from traumatic experiences.

I began writing *Via Chicago* as I surveyed the dramatic changes that have taken place in my own life over the past decade. As someone who has done academic work, teaching, and advocacy related to trauma recovery, I sought to capture the complexity of such experiences as well as the ways these experiences impact the life course. I further sought to highlight the ways social support and the connections we develop with others influence how we see and respond to traumatic past experiences over time. Further, as a bisexual, transgender, and polyamorous person who has written on, taught about, and experienced diverse forms of "family" over time, I sought to capture how people construct chosen families of varied types in relation to their own needs, experiences, and desires as individuals and in collaboration with others. Throughout the pages of *Via Chicago*, each of these themes find voice.

I also wanted to explore the importance of place in our sense of who we are, where we fit (within families, cultures, or otherwise), and how we experience the world. Although I often write about and do research focused on the southeastern United States, Chicago is one of my favorite places and the place I have most often gone to recharge, relax, think, and process in the past decade. In fact, I am so familiar with the city that locals and others often mistake my discussions of the place as evidence of long term residence at some point. Seeking to capture this feeling of "being at home" or a part of a place, whether or not one lives there, I set the story in Chicago while utilizing many references to places in the city that I hold dear and that have been the site of important moments in my life. My hope is that readers might reflect on what places matter most to them, and why that might be.

As such, I close this preface with a handful of questions that readers might consider while following the lives captured in *Via Chicago*. Since this novel could be utilized in the teaching of sociology, families, romantic relationships, gender, sexualities, geography, urban studies, LGBTQIA studies, polyamory, trauma recovery, or narrative courses, I would ask students in these classes to think about what a family is and what it means to be one; what trauma is and how traumatic experience influences the life course; and where they feel most at home and what that says about themselves and these places. *Via Chicago* can, of course, also be read entirely for pleasure, but even in such cases, I would suggest readers consider how their own families, relationships, and experiences relate to those that unfold throughout this book.

ACKNOWLEDGEMENTS

Thank you to Patricia Leavy, John Bennett, Jolanda Karada, and everyone else at Brill | Sense and the *Social Fictions* series for your faith in me, your willingness to support creativity, and your invaluable guidance. I would also like to especially thank Shalen Lowell for your considerable assistance and support. I cannot overstate how much the efforts and support of all you means to me. Thank you to everyone at Brill | Sense for supporting this book and my growth as an author.

Thank you especially to my spouse Xan Nowakowski for giving me the courage to write novels in the first place and walking by my side as I completed them and sent them out for consideration. My books would not exist without your inspiration, guidance, and faith, and I will never be able to thank you enough for what your support and encouragement means to me.

I would also like to thank Lain Mathers, Nik Lampe, Eve Haydt, Shay Phillips, Brittany Harder, Mandi Barringer, Dawne Moon, Katie Acosta, and Eric Anthony Grollman for providing constructive comments and insights throughout this process and my life in general. There is no way for me to express how important each of you are to everything good about my life and writing.

Further, I would like to express my gratitude to some people I have only met once in passing after a concert. This work was written while I listened nonstop to Wilco, and their records, as they did while I was in college and later writing a dissertation, provided the soundtrack for the writing, editing, and revision of the work.

Finally, this novel would not be possible without the years of research I have done on sexualities, gender, religion, and health. I have had the privilege of interviewing and observing so many wonderful LGBTQIA people over the years, and many of their experiences find voice in this novel. I would thus like to thank all of them both for sharing their stories with me.

MERCURY

I remember clearly the moment she confessed her undying love to me.

We were supposed to just be meeting for coffee like we had a few times before that uncharacteristically warm February morning in 2018. We were supposed to be catching up on everything that had happened since we last saw each other when I passed through the city she lived in at the time for work. We were supposed to be talking about what it was like to be getting used to the patterns of life in Chicago. We were supposed to be celebrating her latest novel, which she promised to give me an autographed copy of that day. We were supposed to be trading notes about places to eat, grab coffee, or just have a good time now that we were both going to be living here. We were not, however, supposed to change everything I thought I knew about who and what we were or could be.

She was not supposed to look up from the new novel she was signing for me, and say, "I feel like you should know that I'm attracted to you."

She was not supposed to say that. That was not supposed to happen. She was supposed to sign the book, make some self-deprecating remark about her writing, and then resume the normal chit chat of our previous conversations. She was not supposed to say eleven words that seemed to take all the breath out of my lungs. That is not what was supposed to happen. I would have been more prepared for a fire breathing dragon to suddenly fly out of her beautiful soft blue eyes and start talking to me in Arabic than I was for her to say those eleven words before looking back down at the book she was signing at a Peet's Coffee on Michigan Avenue.

"I, ugh, I," I stuttered like a damn fool! I would like to lie to you right now and say that I said something magical, beautiful, or at least grammatically correct. I did not. If I'm being completely honest with you, I thought I was going to pass out on the spot.

You have to understand that I thought I was dreaming. I thought I was having a mental breakdown where I could not tell my dreams from reality. I was waiting to wake up. I had envisioned the moment she declared her love for me in the past. I imagined it the first time I saw her as she discussed her first novel in an old building at Agnes Scott College when I was just an undergraduate student uncertain of what the hell to do with my life. Hell, at the time my life was so terrible I wasn't even sure I wanted to do anything with it. I imagined it each time we traded emails after she seemed so nice at the meet and greet following her talk. I imagined it when we met for coffee whenever I could find a way – or make one up – for school or work or my private life to get me to Miami where she lived before moving to Chicago. I imagined it many other times in many different ways, but I never thought it would happen.

The truth is, though I don't like sharing this with you, that I never expected this fantasy to walk into reality. You have to understand that I did not see myself as a full person at the time. After a handful of traumatic events, I saw myself more like a cartoon or a stick figure. I was not the type of thing that people loved or were attracted to. I was definitely not the type of thing that a novelist would find desirable. I honestly thought we struck up what I, while laughing at myself I admit, thought of as our friendship because she found me amusing or entertaining in some way like a display at one of those circus of freaks attractions it seems like so many carnivals have for some reason I've never understood. I was not attractive, as far as I could imagine, so how in the hell could this woman be attracted to me?

You also have to understand that, well, I would have never imagined that this particular woman could find anything, and I mean anything, even interesting about me in the first place. I mean, come on, she was married to one of the smartest, sexiest, and most amazing people I had ever met. Oh yeah, did I mention that she has a spouse? Yes, she does. An amazing rock star of a spouse to tell you the whole truth. The kind of spouse that could make any hero or heroine from one of them fantasy stories quiver with insecurity from head to toe. I'm not joking, that's how amazing they are, at least! I remembered reading her second novel, the one that contained a relationship like her own and how they practiced nonmonogamy, and simply drooling about even the thought of being near people like them. I admit I had more than a few dreams while I devoured that novel, but come on, what in the hell would people like that want with a stick figure like me? I just couldn't imagine it.

"I hope I didn't upset you," she says smiling at me and probably noticing that my entire face is about as red as a stop sign. I think I'm shaking. Am I shaking? When will I wake up? There is no way this is real. I've had WAY TOO MUCH to drink this time. I mean, I haven't had anything to drink this time, but it feels like I must have gotten wasted again without realizing it, that's the only other explanation that makes as much sense as dreaming, right? "I don't want you to think that anything ever needs to happen between us," she says, and I feel my heart sink. I want to scream PLEASE at the top of my lungs, but instead I just continue my impression of a stop sign because I can't remember how to speak or think or anything else. "I just felt like you should know since we may continue to have these little coffee dates, if you're comfortable with that, and I don't think it would be fair for me to be attracted to you at such times and you have no clue that I may be thinking of you in those kinds of ways. Does that make sense?"

For a moment, I was glad I couldn't talk. I would have told her that nothing made sense anymore. I would have asked her where the dragon was and when it would fly out of her beautiful eyes to laugh at me and set the coffee shop on fire. This felt plausible, or at least as plausible as her wanting me, could she really want me? I would have, shit, I don't even know what I would have done or said. I finally did find my voice and managed to cough and pick up my already empty coffee cup. She smiled at me again. I felt like I was going to melt. I felt like I was going to explode. I felt like I had to be dreaming, I just had to be. I was sure of it. I just had to be dreaming. After what seemed like twenty years, I muttered, "Um," and ducked my head because for some reason my voice reminded me of a dying cat, "Um, okay, well, I should be, ugh, I guess, getting home because, ugh, well, um, it's getting kind of late."

At this point, I was relatively certain she would, at least, laugh at me if not say something incredibly mean. I mean, come on, what the hell kind of response was that? I still want to lie to you and say I came up with something else, but that was it. I got up from the table.

She smiled at me. That was it. Nothing mean, no laughter, just a damn smile. I grabbed the book she had finished signing for me. I almost dropped it twice, but I didn't. That was a stroke of luck that further convinced me I was definitely dreaming. She smiled again. I wanted to kiss that smile, but I was sure I would pass out if I did. I muttered something, I think, and then I left.

I would like to tell you for sure that I did not run away at an embarrassing speed. I would like to tell you that, but to this day I'm still not sure if that would be completely honest.

ELLA

"I told Collette I needed her," I cried to Case as we sat at the stone table outside of a classroom building in August of 2011.

Both of those moments stand out to me as I think about everything that has happened. I told Case that I told Collette, "I need you." I said that to Collette in a cheap motel in Long Beach, Mississippi at the end of the Fall of 2008. If I'm being completely honest with you, I have to admit that I had never said those words to another human being before that night. I mean, of course I felt like I needed people plenty of times before that night. I just never told anyone. It seemed too honest, too real. I don't know why I told Collette. I really don't. I don't even know why I said that to Case sitting outside that night in 2011. I know that, back in 2008, I felt so isolated during that first semester of graduate school at the University of Miami. I know that I felt like Collette understood me better than anyone because we both grew up in Long Beach and wanted out with all we had. I know that right before I said those words, she said that if I told her I needed her she would go with me back to Florida for my second semester of graduate school.

"I don't understand Ella," Case said on that night in 2011 while wiping some of the tears that had accumulated on my face while I sobbed like a newborn someone hugged too tight in the delivery room, "What are you talking about, what's wrong?"

I remember trying to figure it out in the moment. I wanted to be able to answer Case since they were putting up with me in about the most vulnerable moment of my life at that point. Maybe one of those things led me to say what I really felt at the time. Maybe it was something else. I don't know, but that moment still sings in my mind as the moment when all this began. I guess that's why I told Case about it that night in 2011 even though we barely knew each other at that point. I remember that in 2008 I was living in Florida working on what I planned to be a doctorate in literature. I was so broke that I would have had to save up to be poor. I was just getting used to being myself, the way I always saw myself, and completely different from all the younger people in the graduate program with their kind families and external sources of support. I was scared and alone. That is the overwhelming feeling I have when I think about that first semester of graduate school. Maybe that was it. Maybe I was so scared and alone that I was left with no other choice than to tell someone how I really felt about something, anything maybe.

Hell, maybe that's the same reason I let Case see me cry and why I told them about that moment with Collette in the first place. I don't know, but I turned to Case, feeling the sting in the corners of my eyes, and said, "I can't be alone anymore, I don't remember how!"

I don't know how to explain how terrible that realization felt in 2011. I don't know, but I know that after those words left my mouth, I wanted them back like a calm summer breeze just before a thunderstorm. I wanted it to be a dream or a delusion or a nightmare or whatever, just not real. I didn't want to feel that way. I didn't want to need anyone. I made it through the abuse of a childhood, the death of lovers, the violence that seemed to find me no matter where I went, I made it through all of that by learning to be alone, to not feel things, to just survive one day at a time. I didn't want to need anyone, but I knew when I said those words to Case that they were true. They were just as true as the words I said to Collette in 2008. I hated it. I hated me. I hated everything and everyone and words coming from my own traitor of a mouth most of all and more than anything I could imagine at the time.

"Oh Ella," Case said wrapping their left arm around my shoulder. I can't believe I let them. "It's going to be okay. I know you miss Collette, but the relationship wasn't working out for either of you."

I remember that right after I told Collette I needed her she said she loved me. I said I loved her too. This surprised me both because I said it and because I meant it. She went with me to Florida when I left at the end of the break. We were married only a few months later. Getting married meant that she could stay in school and finish her undergraduate degree in Florida. It also meant we had a better financial situation alongside our two, though later only one, incomes.

It also meant that for the first time I could remember, the fact that I was misdiagnosed as male at birth came in handy because it allowed us to access the financial benefits of legal marriage. We were good together, but like one cup of ice cream at a buffet, not enough. Two years later, we were separating, and I was crying on a stone table in front of Case and wanting to die because I felt more aware of just how alone I was than I ever remembered feeling.

"I don't know what to do," I sobbed in a voice that reminded me of the worst squeals from the most terrible heavy metal album ever created. Case pulled me closer. I let them for some reason I still can't comprehend. I didn't really let people touch me back then. I also didn't talk much back then. I couldn't remember the last time I had cried as I sat there on a stone bench in front of classroom building in Miami in 2011.

"I don't know either," Case said, and I remember wishing they had an answer of some sort, "But I know it will be okay. You'll be okay Ella, you just have to hang on to that truth until you can feel it yourself like you told me the first time I came by your office."

I stared at them through the haze of a new set of tears that came softer and slower than the last batch. It was like there was one of those pumps that controls a koi pond somewhere inside my face, and it was rationing out the water. For a moment, they didn't look like the goofy neighbor that lived below me in a beat-up apartment building designed to remind the poor students just how poor we really were. For just a second, they looked like the scared student that showed up at my office after the first course they took with me holding an extra credit essay assignment where they had expressed what it felt like to suffer through a traumatic event for the first time. I saw that scared student blend with my fun neighbor who chain smoked cigarettes and still had nightmares like two threads of fabric building a quilt. "I don't know if I'm strong enough to do that Case."

"I still don't know if I am," Case said chuckling the way they do at a particularly nerdy scene in a *Family Guy* episode, "But I trust you so maybe you can trust me when I say I'm sure you're strong enough to do it."

LINSK

"There was a part of me that didn't think you would come to Chicago," I said to Ella as we sat on the back porch of our apartment in Logan Square.

I was running my long fingers against the edge of my wine glass like I often do when I'm nervous about something. I was thinking about my parents again. I've done that a lot in the years Ella and I have spent together. I was thinking about the pain of growing up alone after they died. I was thinking about how even having a career, desires in general, or anything just felt, well, unthinkable for so long. I was thinking about what it felt like when I took my dream job here in Chicago six months before I said these words to Ella in November of 2017. I was doing my best to make sure I didn't give myself a hard time for doubting she would travel across the country to be with me. On some level, I knew she would follow me to the end of the earth. She said so more than once. She meant it. I knew she meant it. At the same time, sometimes it can be really hard to believe in the good things after you've seen and survived terrible things. As Reeves put it one day, "after a lifetime alone, sometimes it's hard to adjust to being an us."

"There is nowhere I would rather be Linsk," Ella said twirling her hair the way she does when she's talking about anything important.

I remember when we met she barely spoke. She would just say random words and write me these long letters. She was in a doctoral program for literature that she quit after publishing her first novel in 2012. I was working on my own doctorate in public health. We met the first day of my doctoral program. She was sitting in an orientation for graduate students because she had been assigned to try to mentor an asshole guy in the psychology department that later left to work with so called men's rights movements. I was there because all the new graduate students had to go to the orientation even if we already had graduate degrees. I remember the first time I saw her, soft red hair that somehow fit the skirt she was wearing like a perfectly crafted mix tape. It was like she was lit with a different kind of light than the rest of the people in the room.

"I know you really mean that," I said smiling. "I love the new job, and I can't wait to take you to the health center, so you can meet everyone and see where I work."

"I would love that," she says smiling back at me.

I'm still getting used to her new appearance. She is losing weight now that she isn't in so much pain all the time. We have walked through so much pain together. Much of it was mine, much of it was hers, together we somehow always make it, and she smiles a lot now. She didn't used to smile. Years ago, some asshole attacked her on a street and the damage to her face was severe. I remember that when we met in late 2011, I was drawn to the way her face and mouth seemed so different than other people I had known. I remember walking through a supermarket one afternoon and asking her what happened. I remember how scared and shy she looked as we stood there. When she told me about the attack, it looked like she was trying to be ready for another one. I'll never forget that look. It broke my heart. I remember cradling her face and telling her she was beautiful. She choked up at the sound of those words. I did too. It was one of so many moments over the past few years, but it always comes to mind when I think about the life we've built together.

"Do you miss Florida," I ask as she lights a cigarette and blows out a stream of smoke that dances along the edge of the porch where my plants will grow in the spring and summer. I'm looking forward to having plants again. When I got here earlier in the year, I was too busy setting up my office, getting to know the other researchers I would be working with, and just embracing my new job to think much about them. When we lived in Miami, I always had flowers. They were with me, and later with us, all year round every year. There is something about watching them grow that speaks to the growth in my own life. It reminds me that I am never finished becoming who I am. It reminds me that the lack of completion is not only okay, but natural and necessary and welcome at the same time. It reminds me to breathe a little deeper when I can and take a moment to reflect on all I've seen and done in my life.

"A little bit," she says laughing, "Especially in this cold. How about you?"

Ella has never expressed any desire to live in cold climate. She said she always saw herself as a lifelong southern belle when we met, but I guess the way we see ourselves can change when the reason for the transformation is important enough. I always saw myself as just a sick person or just an orphan, but these days I realize just how much more I am than any one characteristic. Ella helped me with that the same way I helped her learn to smile. Like right now, she's wearing a Chicago Bulls hoodie and sitting in a new home in a new city that is far removed from the south. Something about that says something important about commitment the same way the plants I grow tell me things by their mere presence. She holds her coffee cup against her cheek for a moment. She doesn't know why she does this when I've asked, but it's one of the little mannerisms that make her who she is.

"I do," I say matching her laugh, "And I could definitely live without the cold."

I never thought much about the possibility of living in a cold climate either. I don't know if I would have picked Chicago out of a lineup when I was thinking of where my dream job would arise, but the city feels right to me and I know Ella loves this place, has ever since that kind woman gave her pizza long before we found each other. I can relate to that woman. I always wanted to help people. I especially wanted to help people who need help the most. When the health center came calling for a new evaluator who would focus on public service programs for the most marginalized citizens of the Chicagoland area, something about it just spoke to me in a way that makes me feel warm even on the colder nights. I was telling Reeves and Ella about that as I packed to move here. Both of them, in their own ways, suggested that I would regret it way too much if I ignored those feelings. They knew I needed this. Sitting on my new balcony, I have to admit that I knew that already, but it was good to hear it when I needed to hear it from the people who matter most to me.

"Case says we'll get used to it," she says blowing smoke that catches in the cold air and seems to hover above our porch just long enough to enjoy the moment.

"That's what I think," I say trying to remember if I've ever been somewhere so cold for more than a few days. Growing up on the east side of Atlanta with the medical researchers who took me in after my parents passed away, we had winters, but not like this. I remember when Case first moved here in 2012, they thought the winter would kill them. "Reeves says the same, but he was raised in New Jersey before moving south so who knows how comparable that will be for us from the warmer climates."

"I hope they're both right," Ella says giggling in the way she does only when she's especially happy or when I make silly voices that make her, as she puts it, "feel like my heart is too happy for verbiage." I love it when she says things like that. She takes a sip of her coffee from the Gaslight Coffee Roasters place she is already in love with, and says, "Do we know when he'll be able to join us here?"

"Yeah, this morning he got word that the transfer is approved, and he'll be here by the summer at the latest," I say thinking about the potential joy of having both of my spouses under the same roof again. Sometimes it's hard to believe I found so much love after almost dying in my early twenties and spending so many years feeling so alone, and yet, somehow, I did. As Ella continues smoking and looking over the galleys for her new novel, I remember when we met and later when we found Reeves. It's hard to believe the way things work out sometimes. If I'm being completely honest with you, there was a time when I thought I would be much better off never being with anyone in any way other than maybe the occasional casual date or friends-with-benefits kind of thing. I look at Ella sitting with her legs crossed here on the porch during a temporary break from the cold, and I think about talking to Reeves on the phone about his latest series of paintings while I was in the tub last night, and something inside feels even warmer than the best Florida summers have to offer. I may have to wait a few months to grow any more plants, but something special seems to already be growing with a powerful force like a hurricane here in our new city as I watch the soft blue of Ella's skirt sway in the breeze on our new porch.

CASE

I will never forget the combination of pain and joy I felt the first morning I woke up in Chicago what seems like a lifetime ago in 2012.

It is still hard to believe that two years before that morning I was wasting away in undergrad classes I didn't care about and a haze of marijuana smoke that seemed to cover everything. I was going through the motions. I was surviving. I was not alive in the ways I have come to know life. I realize now that I was basically hiding. I was hiding from the sound of the gun shots when my best friend died in front of me in 2008. I was hiding from the nightmares of that moment that I knew would come any night I didn't aid my sleep with more marijuana than likely would have been useful. I was hiding from the fact that I didn't believe I deserved to live, that I felt like I was the one who should have caught the stray bullet. I still feel that way sometimes, but it's not the same as it was then.

Back then, I was a scared kid who didn't know much of anything about the world. I was trying to make sense of death, grief, and the guilt that comes from watching others fall when you are allowed to continue standing for some reason. Of course, that was the problem. I was searching for some reason. Like so many people, I could only create a reason by assuming I had some control over the events that I never had in the first place. The downside of this, of course, was that by imagining I had control I became able to see the events as in some way my fault. If I had control, there was a reason it happened, but if I had control, then that also meant that maybe I could have stopped the event in the first place. I spent so much time trying to figure what one thing I could have done differently to make it all go away. I never found it because it didn't exist, but I tried so hard for so long and felt worse and worse over time.

If I'm being completely honest with you, I have to admit that I didn't want to take the creative writing class that made all the difference. I wanted to take another class with another instructor who I enjoyed previously, but she was not teaching, and she recommended

I take the creative writing class. I guess that class is what changed everything for me. It's funny to realize that I almost didn't get into the class because it filled up so fast, and I didn't want to take the class in the first place. Sometimes I think about what my life might have been like if I had never taken that class. I don't like to think about this, but sometimes I do. I remember that I didn't know what to make of Ella at the beginning of the class. Of course, I didn't call her Ella then. I called her Professor August like all the other students. I didn't know we would somehow become best friends. I didn't know I would finally start facing the aftermath of the shooting in an extra credit assignment. I just knew that she seemed unlike anyone I had ever met before in my life.

I think about that class a lot when I come here to the tea house that Ella says looks like something out of *The Lord of the Rings*. I come here to work on my own graduate studies now. I remember when I arrived in the city, I just went roaming around feeling the air around me. I was riding the red line one day, and I thought it was funny that there was a stop called Chicago. I got off at the stop and started walking. Ella made us read *The Hobbit* in her class that semester in 2010. I remember turning the corner that day in 2012 and seeing this tea house. I think it reminded me of something out of Tolkien's world too. It was August, which seemed fitting because I was already starting to miss Ella. I lived below her my final year of college, and it was harder to say goodbye when I moved than I would have guessed. She wasn't teaching anymore. She had published her novel and moved in with Linsk in a nicer part of Miami. I took a seat in the tea house and wrote in my journal.

I did not mean to come back here after that day, but something about this spot just spoke to me. It would show up in my dreams. It would flash through my mind as I sat through the fascinating and the boring classes that made up my first semester of graduate study. I remember being worried that Ella would forget me when I moved here. I was sure that she would move on with her life, and I would feel all alone again. I was wrong. She felt the same way I did. She thought I would forget about her too. She was wrong as well. I was having trouble writing a paper at the end of my first semester. I was asking Ella what I should do on a phone call that somehow became another ritual. She didn't like phones. She made an exception, she said, because I "sounded really stressed out." After that, we started talking on the phone regularly, often for hours. We still did until she moved here in November. As Jo put it the other day, "Sometimes new rituals come from new people, maybe we begin again with each new person we love." Jo says stuff like that when she's a little high and its late at night and she stops worrying about what she'll do with her life for a few minutes.

I remember Ella told me to think of the most peaceful place I had found in the city. She said that was what I needed for the paper. "Writing," she said, "Requires freedom. You have to just let go, don't try to get it right, just try to get it out. For that," she continued, "Sometimes you need a sense of calm outside of yourself if you cannot find it within yourself." It sounded a lot like trauma instead of writing to me then and now, but I realized that it was both. I told her about this spot. She said I should go there. I said it was wintertime. She didn't understand what that meant. Her inner southern belle sat outside year-round in the Miami sunshine, but Chicago was a long, long way from Miami. I explained that there would be less seating and no real outdoor seating. She said that part didn't matter. I told her it was silly. She said to try it anyway. I remember sitting here the next day. It took forever, or so it seemed, but I wrote my paper. I even got an A on the paper when I submitted it the following Friday.

"We just had to meet here," Ella said as she slid into the chair on the other side of the table from me in November 2017. "It just had to be this place."

I wanted to see her as soon as possible when she got set up in town. She knew this. Linsk knew this. Reeves knew this. Kaisa knew this. Jo knew this. Michelle knew this. Andrei knew this. We all knew this. She slid into the chair that day, and in that moment, her living in the same city I did again felt real. Reunited in the tea shop as fellow residents of the same city, via the Chicago stop on the red line, I stared at her. It wasn't the same as when she would visit me sometimes while still living in Miami or when I would visit her during each winter break. This was different, somehow better. Kaisa rubbed my shoulders in bed one night, and said, "Having her nearby calms you the same way our time together calms you, me, and even our cats – it's something to do with deep love that can't really be explained in any simple way." I kissed Kaisa. They always know the right things to say when I'm working through ideas or feelings or freaking out because I think I left the stove on or forgot to lock the apartment seventeen minutes after leaving for work.

     "I felt like this would be the perfect spot for us to get drinks the first time we did so as fellow residents of Chicago," I said half sticking my tongue out the way I do at Kaisa when I'm trying to be extra cute.

LINSK

"Are you enjoying the juicy muscles," Ella asks on the other end of the telephone.

Laughing, I say, "You know I am, not to mention a little break from the cold."

I'm standing in the kitchen at our old place in Miami, which we still have while Reeves finishes up transferring his gallery business to Chicago. I came down for a visit right after New Year's, and Ella is happy Reeves and I get time together, but jealous that we get to go outside in shorts and t-shirts while she navigates what she called, "Way too much damn cold for any reasonable person." Reeves and I don't have the heart to tell her this is a good winter by Chicago standards. Instead, we just keep sending her pictures of palm trees and beaches because what is life without a little whimsy and the joy of teasing your lovers. Reeves comes out of the bathroom smiling at me, and I giggle at the sight of the juicy muscles I love so much. He kisses me softly on my forehead and moves to the other side of the room to look over some submissions from a young artist who wants to do a show at the gallery.

"Did I tell you Mercury moved into the city," Ella says after a few more comments about the juicy muscles.

When I first referred to Reeves' juicy muscles after meeting him at a gallery opening in Hannibal Square in Orlando in 2014, Ella thought it was the cutest phrase in the world. She said I should call him on the ninth day in a row I brought him up after returning from the Orlando trip. We always talk about and clear anyone else before they can become involved with one or both of us sexually, romantically, or in both ways. Reeves was cleared very quickly because, as she put it at the time, Ella could tell, "That there seems to be something special for you there, honey." I remember I gave him a call thinking that it would be no big deal. Sometimes the little, as I thought of them at the time, side dates beyond what Ella and I have were fun, but they rarely led to much more than fun and a few laughs. As I told Case at the

17

time, it was interesting because it wasn't like Ella or I needed anything beyond ourselves, it was more that we saw no reason to limit what either or both of us could have so we followed wherever our individual or shared desires led at any time just to see what was possible.

"The one from Agnes Scott," I asked still thinking about the feel of Reeves' arms wrapped around me in a Sheraton in Winter Park, Florida that first time, "Are the two of you going to get together for coffee and catch up?"

I was so far off the mark on Reeves that it became a running joke in the family over the years he has been with us. Case finds it especially hilarious because Ella had a similar "I don't know what this is, but what the hell" feeling when she first found me in 2011 after her first marriage dissolved. Reeves was and is, as Case put it, "The absolute opposite of no big deal." There was something about his open emotional expression, his desire to help other people despite having been treated shitty by many people himself, and his juicy muscles that set me on fire in a way that made me feel delirious. The only comparison I have is the way Ella ignites me. That first phone call turned into a series of long calls, short visits, long nights, and wonderful mornings where I learned his body, his experiences growing up in New Jersey and getting into the arts, and his dreams about someday having a family after being mostly alone his whole life. I guess sometimes we don't know there is something more, something missing, until we find it. Ella says that's what happened when I found Reeves and we realized our family needed him as we need each other even though we didn't realize he had been missing until we already had him with us.

I sit down on the couch and Reeves puts his head in my lap as Ella says, "Yeah, they want a copy of my new novel and it would be nice to see them again, so maybe we'll get together in February before my Jacksonville trip."

"A little more than nice, I bet," I say giggling at the feeling of Reeves' soft facial hair rubbing against my stomach, "They seem like someone special to you sweetheart, and I think we both know you're attracted to them even if you don't want to admit that yet."

I run my fingers across Reeves' massive chest and watch him kind of squirm in response to the movements of my long, thin fingers.

He nods his head at the words I'm saying to Ella. We both feel like there is something special to Ella about Mercury, Case does too, but none of us can quite put our finger on what it is. It reminds me of the way Ella talked about what Reeves seemed like in my talks about him back when we met. I don't know if it's the same thing, but it feels similar. Of course, Ella is just as bad as the rest of us at noticing these things for herself. Somehow, despite being so lost and alone as individuals, Case, Reeves, Ella, and I all found each other, "Fellow kicked puppies," as Case's partner Kaisa puts it and knows from their own experiences of abandonment and abuse. We help each other heal and chase dreams that once seemed like utter impossibilities at best.

"I don't know about all that," Ella says laughing in the way that I know from years of experience has more to do with anxiety than humor. I can just see her twirling her hair and lighting a cigarette trying to both think about what I said and avoid thinking about it at the same time. She's probably cuddled up in the University of Miami blanket we keep draped over the couch shaking her head and blushing at the same time. I smile thinking about my own similar moments like this over the years when this or that person caught my attention and I wasn't sure just what, if anything, it meant or was going to lead to in the end.

"You should think about it honey," I say smiling and then I softly kiss Reeves on the forehead and feel the smile radiating throughout his body at my touch.

JO

"You really are the worst smoker ever, aren't you," I ask Mercury as they try for the ninth time to light a cigarette on North Clybourn.

I met Mercury when we were in separate classes and separate years at Agnes Scott College in Atlanta, Georgia. They were planning to be an exercise scientist of some sort before finally figuring out that they preferred public health research. I was planning to be the trophy wife of a business man before realizing I had a thing for marketing and public relations. I was in my second to last year at the college, and already looking forward to leaving Atlanta behind the same way I left the beach town on the west coast of Florida after high school. They were in their first year at the college, and something about the joy they had freshly transplanted to Atlanta spoke to me when we met at an event put on by some religious student group they were part of at the time. I was just there for the free food and to make jokes under my breath about the religious people; everyone needs a hobby I always say.

"You of all people know that I'm not much of a smoker, but I'm so nervous about graduate school coming up in the fall and getting used to the city and other stuff," Mercury says running their hand through the peach fuzz on the top of their head that somehow accentuates the dimensions in their face better than any of the other haircuts they've had since I've known them.

"And by other stuff you mean your recent conversation with a certain thriller-writing novelist we both know," I ask knowing the answer already.

This is something you get used to when talking to Mercury. There are few direct conversations when emotions come into play. It is more like putting together a crossword puzzle like my terrible mother used to do at the kitchen counter in between tirades about how much weight I should lose or how useless my inquisitive child mind was for anything practical in this world. I think about my upcoming graduation. I think about the master's degree I almost have. Take that mom! I think about the nice apartment I have in the heart of Chicago, and the fun I have doing promotion for writers and artists for a living. Yeah, take that mom! Mercury and I bonded early on due to the fact that we were both trying to escape where we came from and trauma that came with those old, ghost-filled places.

"Wouldn't you be nervous about that," they say in a tone more defensive than necessary. Of course, that is what they were really talking about, but it annoys them when I pick up on the things in between what they say directly, about as much as I enjoy it.

"Of course, I would, but I just find it funny you didn't mention it specifically in the list you took the time to create just now," I say sticking my tongue out at them.

They finally get their cigarette lit and we start walking down North Clybourn. There is a noodle place we both like this way, and I'm too hungry to not have noodles even though I didn't find the book I wanted at the Barnes & Noble. Of course, it would help if I knew what book I was looking for in the first place. I'm always looking for it, but the quest remains unfulfilled. I feel like one day I have to find the one that makes my heart pump so hard I throw the damn thing across a room at a climactic moment, but I'm still waiting. It reminds me, sadly, of my sex life to date, but what are you going to do. If I'm being completely honest with you, I have to admit that I pay so much attention to my friends and my books because my own life often feels more boring than I would like to admit to myself on the nights when I'm all alone and out of weed.

"I just don't know what to do about it Jo, that's my problem, I just don't know. I've spent the past few days re-reading her novels thinking maybe there is an answer in one of them. I even got into an argument at a coffee shop with some asshole who thought her novel about the guy who killed people who made fun of his writing was some kind of metaphor for conservatism and I've barely slept all week, I just don't know what to do," they say tossing the cigarette before it even reached the halfway-smoked point as they often do.

"You got it bad, don't you," I say laughing and thinking about how Mercury became a smoker who is not really a smoker and maybe the worst smoker ever.

They were looking for ways to make money their last semester of college. They found a flyer for a psychology study on smoking habits. They sent me the flyer. I still have it. It looks like something out of an old book on poorly designed promotion materials to my newfound publicist eyes. It said you could make up to five hundred dollars by smoking and letting the researchers record some aspects of your smoking experience. Mercury didn't make five hundred dollars. They couldn't smoke enough to do that. They made two hundred. They did this by walking into a gas station in the Little Five neighborhood in Atlanta and asking for a pack of cigarettes. They didn't know anything about the types, so they just asked for the kind they saw hipsters smoking and picked the prettiest box of that brand. It is a light blue. I see it popping out the back pocket of their jeans right now. They couldn't make themselves a five-hundred-dollar smoker, but they did get two hundred that paid for a few meals and a cell phone bill along the way. Maybe not the success the researchers anticipated, but a success, nonetheless.

"You can just leave," Mercury says in response to my joke, and I start giggling. I point to the noodle place when I can see the sign and stop to move a piece of my sometimes annoying though equally invaluable to me brown hair out of my eyes. They nod.

"You can just call her," I say as we enter the noodle place.

"Yeah, that's what I'll do. I'll just call her, all cool and whatever, I can see it now. 'Hey Ella, I know I ran away like a squirrel when we met for coffee, but that was because I'm like so in love with you I can't stand it, so, like, you wanna hook up?"

"Whatever," I say in between bursts of laughter. The guy behind the counter looks at us like we're crazy. I guess everyone is a little crazy, but most of the time the people who serve us noodles don't seem to notice. I wonder what it feels like when they do notice. I think about asking him, but Mercury starts talking again.

"It doesn't matter anyhow, she's in Jacksonville talking about her novels," Mercury says running their hands through the peach fuzz on the top of their head, "She won't be back until next week."

"I'm pretty sure they have phones in Jacksonville," I say after they order their noodle dish and before ordering my own.

We take a seat on the edge of the restaurant beside the wall. I remember sitting here one night with Case and Kaisa when I first arrived in Chicago. I met them through contacts from college, and we bonded over a shared, maybe overly critical, view of the world. We sat here that night after going to the Barnes & Noble. I was curious about Case's best friend who is also the novelist Mercury and I are talking about today as we meet for the first time now that we both live in Chicago the same way we would meet up when we both lived in Atlanta. I wonder at the similarity of the moment for a second, but I'm too hungry to think much about it.

At the time, I had no clue that I would somehow find a family that actually loved me simply by having dinner with Case and Kaisa on one of my early nights in this new city, but I guess we never know what is coming, no matter how hard I try to, ahead of time. I'm too hungry to think about this right now too. As our noodles arrive, Mercury says, "Shut up, I know they have phones."

"So, call her," I say laughing and at the same time wondering if Ella needs a publicist and planning to ask her next time we hang out or get pizza with the family.

"I'm too embarrassed about how I acted to call her."

"Then, I guess you just have to wait."

MERCURY

The nightmares started again the second night I slept in Chicago.

I say started again because I had them in Atlanta as well, but for a while, I thought maybe they had gone away into whatever abyss the things we don't want may fall into over the passage of time. I was wrong. They came back. It was just a temporary break. It was funny how they seemed even worse than the first wave because I had the temporary break. They came back roaring like a lion, and for a few nights in a row, I wondered how I ever survived the first wave of them right after I got to college. I guess it was the alcohol or maybe the daily grind of classes at Agnes Scott. Or maybe it was Jo and others who took care of me in little ways I only recently started appreciating but needed more than I knew. In any case, they came back that second night as I slept in my new bed in my uptown apartment in the latest city where I would try to escape the past.

Happy New Year, I thought, shivering in the cold of the first day of January 2018 in the middle of the night.

I got out of bed that night and the nights to come. I walked around the small area that was my new apartment. It felt larger than it was. I think that was because it was new. Or maybe it was because I was in Chicago and thus no longer in Atlanta. Or maybe it was because the roaches that lived all over the run-down Atlanta apartment and came out at the worst times were nowhere to be seen in the new Chicago place. It might have also been because it was a bit bigger, but I never bothered to really compare in any empirical way. It just felt bigger as I walked across the main room to the kitchen. I got some ice cream out of the freezer set above the refrigerator. I looked at the clean dishes beside the sink. The dishes made me smile. I like it when things are clean and orderly. I don't know if I always liked this, but ever since things went to shit all those years ago, the order of things matters a lot to me, it comforts me in some way.

I could feel my hands shaking as I sat on the uncomfortable couch that I got from a yard sale in Andersonville the day I was moving into this building on the corner of Lawrence and North Clarendon. I could feel how hot my skin was. It gets hotter in the night when the nightmares come calling to my mind like unwanted guests arriving just before closing down a restaurant. My clothes disappear in my sleep as I try to shake the heat. I wake up naked. Sometimes I remember what I was dreaming. Other times I don't remember anything. When my hands shake, I organize things like records, pens, books, or much more often, my life. I reach for my phone. I open my planner. I plan everything out here. I do this, I know, because it gives me the semblance of order, like an illusion I need to avoid the chaos in my head. I do this, I know, because it allows me to focus on something in the future rather than the pain of the moment or the horror of the past. I do this, I know, because it's all I can do.

An interesting part of being in a new city preparing to start a new program is that I had to craft my own schedule as I planned to move here and arrived here. There is nothing for school until the orientation in the late summer. There is nothing really happening culturally that doesn't require money (don't have much of that at all) or better weather (the winter in Chicago is not built for roaming around the way I could in Atlanta even though it is supposed to be warmer this winter than usual, I checked while planning to come here). I wonder what warmer really means. I wonder what the winter will be like next year. I wonder about a lot of things when I awaken in the middle of the night – anything to distract me from the nightmares in my head.

I look at my planner. I have a coffee date coming up with a professor who is in the public health program I'll be starting at Northwestern in the fall. She wants someone to help with a summer project. I can do that. It will pass some of the time in between nightmares and ice cream. Jo is traveling, but we're supposed to meet up to look at books and maybe get some food, noodles I think she said, next month when she gets back. There is a support group meeting for transgender and non-binary people I am going to at the end of the month. There is a church nearby that helps the poor and serves as a housing site. I scheduled myself to go by there and see about volunteering later this week. There was a flyer on the bulletin board at Everybody's Coffee about a local theatre group, I'm thinking about maybe joining that one as a hobby at least until school starts in the fall and I have more on my schedule than these scary empty spaces.

As I finish the pint of ice cream before realizing I had been eating it while looking at my planner, I see the edge of an American Aquarium album sticking out of the crate where my other records live for the time being. I got the album because it was mentioned in a novel. Not just a novel, I sigh to myself, one of Ella August's novels. This one involved a string of kidnappings in the southeast that no one could seem to figure out. Something about thrillers, I realize, calms the anxiety in my own mind so I pick up the one I got by Celeste Ng while I was at Tall Tales in Atlanta the week before I moved to this city. I start to read, but after a few moments, I find myself staring at the edge of the record again. I pick up my phone, and text Ella to let her know I moved to Chicago, where she now lives, and see if maybe she wants to catch up sometime this month or maybe in February before or after Jo gets back into town and I have someone to talk to that isn't a stranger. I'm pretty sure I'll hear nothing back even though we've had coffee a few times since meeting in Atlanta by accident when she gave a talk at my college.

But maybe she'll text me back and be happy I live here now. Maybe we can be friends who see each other regularly instead of just people passing like trains in the night, in between stops, only a moment to say hello and hop inside from the rest of the world. Maybe, I think, and open my book again. My hands are shaking less. It feels like an eternity since the nightmare woke me up, but I can see by the clock on the wall that it's only been about twenty minutes. I always wonder how time does that, stretch out like some kind of silly putty in the hardest moments and contract like the most poised muscle in the good times. I guess that's a question for another time I think as I lose myself in another book about someone else's pain and the ways they figured out how to make sense of it.

CASE

Did I lock the door? Did I turn off the oven? Did I shut the windows that I never open? These thoughts run through my head as I make my way through Pilsen.

Ella is giving a talk at Pilsen Community Books. I'm supposed to meet her there. I lived in this neighborhood when I first came to Chicago in 2012. I lived off of 18th street in an apartment that I'm pretty sure was not up to code at any time for more than a moment or two. I lived with a rat named Mark who robbed some woman he was dating before skipping out on our rent to some town in Iowa. I think the police found him in Iowa. I also lived with an actual rat that I called Steve because it seemed like a Steve when it spent evenings searching my underwear drawer moving what seemed slow enough to catch until I tried to catch it and it always found warp speed like something out of a space movie and disappeared into the wall. I don't miss either of those rats, but sometimes I miss this neighborhood.

There was a sweet poly foursome that lived over on the main stretch of 18th if you go right off the pink line train stop. I can't remember their names, but one of them was a writer who seemed almost as plagued by his anxiety condition as I am by my own. I wanna say his name was Brandon. I would find him, and he would find me each time we both showed up at the Nitecap Coffee Bar that I noticed on this walk is no longer open. I miss it, but did I miss it before I realized it was gone. I don't know. He would be working on this or that story with one of his partners coming by at times. I would be working on my early graduate courses and loving the panini sandwiches they served. It wasn't the closest coffee shop to the rat apartment, as I think of the place, but it was special.

I only went there sometimes because it was a bit more of a walk. I would go to Pinwheel Records on the way there to see if they had any Wilco or Taylor Swift albums. I wanna say I got the latest Beyonce album there, but that might have been at Reckless in the loop. I don't know. Sometimes the essence of the feeling is more important than the specific details after the fact. Maybe that's why I find myself thinking about the Nitecap Coffee Bar instead of the Jumping Bean where I spent damn near every morning those first three years in Chicago. In practical terms, the Jumping Bean was my coffee place, but the essence of those walks to the Nitecap is something I can't begin to describe. Like last time, I have this thought as I pass the Jumping Bean on my way to the bookstore.

I remember that I gave Ella a t-shirt from the Jumping Bean that they wore so much that the sleeves developed holes and the Spanish lettering on the shirt began to fade. Was that in 2013? I think it was. She was living in Miami with Linsk. Her first book was doing well, and she was planning to come here to talk and sign books in the summer at the University of Illinois Chicago where I still work on finishing my degree. It's so funny to think about it right now, but I was not a reader at all back then. I couldn't have told you the last time I even opened a novel or any book that wasn't assigned in a class. Ella found this sad and hilarious, like some kind of emo song she said I would likely love, something off one of the Dashboard Confessional albums she said, but it just seemed normal to me at the time. I fell in love with Ella's first book, and now I read novels more than the vast majority of people I know. I don't know how that happened, but somehow, it did.

As I arrive at the bookstore, I'm glad to see there are more people here than last time. I've learned from Jo that this is a good sign. What I don't like, however, is that Ella is not here yet. She just flew back in from Jacksonville, and there should have been more time between her arrival at Midway and the book signing. This was an oversight by the current scheduler. Of course, she is her current publicist and scheduler. She needs someone new, this is not work Ella is good at herself and she knows it. I again remind myself to suggest Ella work with Jo instead of doing her own scheduling and publicity. Just as I think this, I see Jo coming out of the bookstore on her phone laughing about something. She weaves through the people, spots me, and then heads in my direction. She is wearing one of those long, flowing raincoat things that only her and Linsk seem to be able to pull off in any way resembling fashionable, maybe it's their small bodies or already overflowing levels of beauty that allow this, but I can't seem to figure it out.

There are so many things I never seem to be able to figure out.

KAISA

The Timatim Salata makes my mouth water in ways that are hard to describe.

I look across the table. It seems like Linsk feels the same way about it. We are eating at one of our usual places; one of our favorites. The Demera Ethiopian restaurant has become a regular meeting spot for us, sometimes with Case along too, since Linsk moved to the city last year. They have just returned from visiting Reeves, and they are excited about him being here soon and loving having Ella in the city full time, though she's in Jacksonville giving a talk. Linsk swallows a beautiful piece of jalapeno. I take a sip of my water. The server comes by to say hello and check in on us again. We both smile. They leave.

I feel a peace I wasn't aware existed at earlier points in my life. I woke up this morning with one of the cats against my back and Case snoring against my stomach. I could feel Case breathing at the same time I could feel the cat purring. I could have gotten up, but I wanted to just enjoy the feeling for a little while. I remember living in a beat up flat in lower Manhattan. I remember hiding in my closet to avoid the fighting in the rest of the cramped apartment. I remember wishing I didn't have to go home for food or sleep or anything else just so I could avoid the latest set of nightmares in daily life that was that house. I remember watching the masses of people moving through the streets. I wanted to just fall in line behind some of them and keep going, just keep going, until I found something better or just something else.

I finally found a form of that peace in college. I went to college in a small town in Ohio where I assumed, life would be so much different. In many ways, it was. College was fun. The trees were so beautiful. The courses opened my mind in new ways. I found myself in many ways. At the same time, the loneliness continued. I felt alone. I didn't fit. I missed the sounds of the street and the crowds of people who I might not be so eager to follow anymore, but who I still wanted to have the option to walk with again as an older me. I would enjoy the classes, playing baseball on the teams, and even some relationships here and there that were a mixture of goods, bads, and everywhere in between. I would do the things you do when you're happy in college, even though I guess I was never happy enough. Something always felt like it was missing. Life was better, but still, not enough in some way I couldn't make sense of at the time.

If I'm being completely honestly with you, I have to admit that I think I only began making sense of it this morning waking up with Case and this afternoon having lunch with Linsk. I listen to Linsk talk about the amazing new position with the health center, and I think about my own position working with underprivileged youth on the southside of the city. I have the same passion they have for my own work. I think about getting the name change forms for a young transwoman this morning. I think about helping a small boy get a spot on the club baseball team in his neighborhood last week. I think about the young mother who needed her prescription usage directions translated last month. Linsk is talking about getting a family over near the Clinton blue line stop into a clinic that can help them, and I smile about the examples I gave earlier in the conversation as we recapped my work of late.

LINSK

I felt like taking a walk after my lunch with Kaisa.

I also wanted a tea. I looked at my phone to remember where I was. A few months in the city, and I was about halfway through my usual practice of mapping every contour of a given place in my own mind. Pleased that I knew exactly where I was, I walked across the street to the Starbucks that Case frequented when they lived in this part of town. They were staying in an apartment building on the corner of Lawrence and Clarendon, I recalled as I crossed Lawrence, opened the door to the Starbucks, and hoped they had tea selections fitting for a walk in the unusually warm February weather. To my surprise, I saw Mercury sitting at one of the tables in the area to the right of the door next to the bank. I thought about going over to say hello after grabbing my tea on the right side of the store, but they were gone by the time I came back. I wondered if maybe they were living in this part of the city. I was curious if they had fun when they met Ella for coffee and what they thought about Ella's confession.

I put these thoughts aside as I grabbed a hot tea, with just a hint of jasmine if I remembered this flavor correctly and headed out onto Lawrence again and made my way to North Magnolia where my mind and phone both said I would turn left. I watched the Lawrence bus Case and Kaisa took between their respective apartments until they moved in together this past fall splash water everywhere as it passed me. I turned onto North Magnolia and found myself staring at a woman who bared a striking resemblance to pictures of my mother I saw as a child. When I was younger, these kinds of moments felt like flashbacks riddled with potential landmines. I would become emotional and numb at the same time. I would sometimes forget what I was doing for a moment. I would stare at the person wondering if maybe we were related in some distant way like people who find their families on street corners in Disney movies or Broadway shows with far too much singing.

As I passed Leland and later Wilson, I thought about the differences between then and now. Back then, I had no family. I always felt like it was just me against the world. I never really bothered to even consider the possibility that I would ever have anyone because it seemed like that was just setting myself up for failure. I do not accept failure. I also don't invite it. There are things that have no place in my world. Failure is one. Family seemed like one back then, but I guess some things can find a place in a life when they come to matter enough. As I passed a place called, interestingly in my opinion, Broncho Billy Park, I remembered those early days where I was suspicious of everything Ella or Case did, said, or even maybe thought. I didn't realize it then, but there was some part of me that had trouble accepting that others could love me just as I was. I guess I thought I was damaged or broken or something.

I also knew that was unusual, but I always thought that I was a problem. They did not agree. My tendency to plan everything, they found cute. My difficultly ever being limited in any way for any reason, they found inspiring. My need to clean everything to the point where hospital inspectors in a lab would call it overkill, they found charming. My desire to spend a lot of time alone with my books and thoughts and dreams, they thought was part of how I was so successful in my career and something I should never trade for anything in the world. It was so strange. These things and everything I thought was difficult or wrong about me, well, they thought these things were what made me myself instead of just some other person. Reeves put it well a couple years later, "You said it yourself, who would want you to be someone else when they are desperately interested in knowing and spending time with you."

For no particular reason, I turned right on Montrose in front of the Graceland Cemetery. I somehow thought I remembered Ella going to a donut shop near this cemetery years ago on a visit to see Case. "I really needed a three-a.m. coffee, and that is never easy to find in the Midwest," she said laughing on the phone about her adventure that night. I wondered if I had the right cemetery. I think so. It was nice to know exactly where it is for my mental map, but I did not feel like walking through it at the moment even though I think I might do so sometime in the future. Next time, I said to myself and smiled. There would be a next time, after all, since I live here now, and not only that, both Ella and Reeves consider this home, "Any place you are," as Ella put it while Reeves nodded one night in the fall, and Kaisa and Case and even Jo were planning to stay here now too. Michelle and Andrei are still figuring out what they'll do, but maybe they'll stay and if not, we'll visit, and they will too. I stopped. I smiled. This was home now, I thought. That is what it feels like. This is home. They are my home and I am theirs.

Chuckling at the realization, I decided it might be fun to ride on some trains for the hell of it. I had a great book about a group of people in a library written by Sue Halpern. I could ride the trains and read my book. That seemed like a great way to spend the rest of this afternoon. My mental map told me the Montrose brown line stop was not far, and while it would be faster to take a car or a bus transfer from the brown line, I decided I would ride the brown line into the loop and then jump on the blue line back out to our place, yes, our place, in Logan Square. At that moment, my phone went off, and I saw a text from Ella saying, "I kind of miss the trains, boo cars, damn Jacksonville, miss you!" Laughing, I headed for the Montrose stop.

ELLA

I am never too tired to go to Pizano's for deep dish pizza.

I was beyond exhausted after spending three days meeting college students, professors, and book vendors in Jacksonville. It was even more tiresome because there was news throughout the city about more black transwomen getting killed in the city at the time. I was even sleepier than I would have been because I had to hop a car from Midway to go straight to a book signing in Pilsen. I don't know why, but my bones felt like they were tired by the time I arrived at the bookstore to find Jo and Case standing outside chatting. The book signing was fun, or fun experienced through the haze of desperately wishing to be home in bed, but afterward, my little lizard brain screamed for my ritual at a volume louder than a heavy metal enthusiast would have been comfortable with even in the midst of the most kickass shred solo ever.

Ever since I first came to Chicago in 2004 when I ended up here accidentally in the midst of a combined cocaine and Jack Daniels and anonymous sex bender, I have always gone to Pizano's for pizza. This was because that first time I was in the city I realized, at some point while roaming around the loop and wondering what city I was in during a rare moment of lucid sobriety, I had no money and it was fucking cold as hell. I stepped into the building where Pizano's is just looking for a moment of warmth, and I guess that's exactly what I found. The woman with the pigtails and the novelty bow in her hair asked how many as if I was a patron about to eat at the restaurant. I looked down at my dirty hair in my face, smeared makeup, beat-up-so-much-most-other-homeless-people-wouldn't-wear-them clothes, and bleeding left hand. I was amazed she had not called the police on sight and trying to figure that out.

It all started when the guy I met and somehow followed to Chicago turned out to have a partner back in Chicago at his flat who arrived back home sooner than expected. I admit that I followed him in the first place, I now recall, because I was out of money at the time and

39

he had a nice stash of cocaine that he took his eyes off of each time he came so hard he passed out. Somewhere in this story I'm sure there is a moral about not going to random midwestern cities with strange men you just met in train station bathrooms even if you did then spend two days in their hotel room in the city you were passing through stealing some of their coke while using other portions of it with them when they were awake. I'm sure there is a moral there, but I'm too tired to think of it. His partner or whatever he was looked like the size of a tank and seemed equally violent as he threw me against the wall. I took that as my cue to leave.

I wiped my face as the server or whatever she was in the novelty t-shirt said sir hesitantly then mam even more hesitantly. I wasn't surprised to see the blood on my hand. I didn't know what to say so I just said I was getting out of the cold and I would get out of her way. She smiled at me for some reason I still can't understand, handed me some napkins (probably for the blood), and pointed to the side of the main entry where I was standing. "You can sit over there where we serve slices and handle to-go orders," she said with the same smile that didn't seem nearly as evil as most of the smiles I had seen on the faces of servers when my poverty and experience with violence was so obvious to a casual observer. I nodded. I didn't know what else to do. I figured maybe she wanted me to wait there for the police. I sat in the window for three hours. She brought me a free slice of pizza and then another after the first one disappeared faster than a long note in the middle of a pop song's bridge. She also gave me water. I sat there wondering what the hell this place was and stared out of the window wondering what to do.

Five nights later, my fifth night sitting in the window of the pizza place, she asked me what I was doing in the city. I told her I was staying with some other people I found in Uptown, but I didn't have the cash to get back home. I didn't tell her I didn't have a home. I didn't tell her the place in Uptown was the space under a bridge where myself and others set up tents at night and hoped that we would not get hurt as we tried to sleep. I didn't tell her how I got to the city. I didn't tell her I only ended up in the restaurant the first night because I ran out of cocaine I had stolen from a guy with a cute ass whose partner beat the shit out of me. I just told her I was pulling little odd jobs here and there to get some bucks to get home. She asked me how much it cost to get home. I told her since I had been repeating the number like a mantra for days and had it handy in the front of my mind. At the end of her shift that night, she gave me the money for the bus ticket that would take me back toward the areas of the country I knew more at the time. I never saw her again. I never thought I would come to Chicago again. I left the next day.

These images or memories or snapshots or whatever you want to call them ran through my head as Case, Jo, and I ordered a deep dish pizza, cheese only, we could split after the book signing. This happens every time I enter the restaurant. Before moving to the city, I came here on every visit and sometimes Case would sit in the window like I did years before in between those visits because they said it felt like my spirit was there in building. It was a way to be close to me when geography would not allow physical proximity. I do the same thing sometimes now that I live in the city. I just come by and sit in the window with a slice of pizza. I think about the girl who was nice to a beat-up, bloody, addict all those years ago. I think about just how good a slice of pizza can taste when you can't remember the last time you ate. I think of the tent city that I'm fairly sure most people in the city never notice or know is there in the first place a few miles north of the restaurant. I think about how different my life is all these years later, and what a difference meeting Collette, then Case, then Linsk, then Reeves, then Jo, then Kaisa, then Michelle, then Andrei made in my life. I think about the kid at the bookstore in Jacksonville who said I was an inspiration. I wonder what the me who first entered this restaurant would think of that.

On the other side of the table, Linsk was already digging into their salad. Kaisa was ordering their gluten-free pasta. In my own imagination, Reeves was sitting beside Linsk digging into his own salad as I know he will be soon. Our deep dish arrived, and the server cut slices for Jo, Case, and me like they always do here. At that moment, smiling the way she does when something big has happened in her life, Michelle came bouncing up to the table with Andrei smiling softly behind her. They were at a concert in Millenium Park when they heard we were here. They each take their seats, and for just a moment within the busy day-to-day of the broader world, the current incarnation, minus Reeves who is certainly thinking about us down in Miami on this night, of our family sits together laughing as Andrei tells us about the latest crazy television show he is in love with and Michelle blends into the story, the way couples in sync with each other so often do, by providing commentary on each scene he mentions each time he takes a breath or another sip of his Moscow Mule. I watch Michelle put her arm around Kaisa, and I feel Andrei and Case on either side of me.

I look at the seat Reeves will one day fill, and for some reason I look at the ninth chair on the end of the table and wonder if someone, maybe Mercury I think with a laugh, belongs there as well. I smile at the people I love. I listen to them talk. I remember just how lonely Chicago felt that first time all those years ago, about as lonely as the rest of my life did. I wonder what the me that first walked into this restaurant would say about this as well.

JO

I'm not sure how you can fall in love on Twitter, but I guess it's not any crazier than the rest of my life to date.

The wall of my apartment seems to scream at me. I know, I know, silly wall, I will get to you I promise. The damn thing looks like something out of one of those criminal investigation shows. There are pictures and strings all over the place. Ella hired me as her new publicist. I have a map of her novelist career on the wall. It helps me visualize things. I wonder how I'm so organized in my career, now that I and the wall think about it, when my apartment looks like one of those disaster movies that I loved so much when I was in college. I step over the pile of sweaters that I still cannot decide is either already washed or not washed yet or too dirty to bother washing again and almost trip over the open peanut butter jar on the floor beside them. Damn peanut butter! Yes Jo, the peanut butter is the problem in this organizational scheme. Shut up Jo, I think and chuckle. Okay, let's see. They do book talks, but we could get them more of these in Chicago and otherwise. They do the social media thing, but they're horrible at it. I should take that over and maybe do some of that quote art stuff I like. I bet I'm good at that. Get out of the way, I say to the pile of pants that I'm certain I washed the other day and start chuckling again. I need more wine. I didn't buy enough wine to think about laundry tonight. I wonder if the peanut butter is still good, one way to find out.

"Hello," I say after my phone tells me Mercury is calling.

"Hey Jo, do you want to maybe have dinner Saturday, I'm trying to set up my schedule for the week."

"Sounds cool, why didn't you come to Ella's book signing, you said you were thinking about it the other day when we got noodles."

"I don't, well, it's whatever, I didn't think it would be okay."

"Why wouldn't it be okay," I say laughing at the moment I realize the peanut butter is not, in fact, still good. Shit, I think, I need more peanut butter and more wine.

"I don't know, it's fine, it's okay."

43

"Okay Mercury, whatever, anyway, you should have come, we had a blast and now I'm Ella's new publicist, so we should so celebrate when we get dinner!" I stare at the wall. I think Ella's website could be better. She admits she is kind of clueless about selling things. She said I could have total control and do whatever I want. This should be fun. I light a joint. I should clean my apartment, or at least put away the clothes on the floor. I'll do it later. I check Twitter. He's posting again. How does he come up with such funny stuff? I don't know. We are supposed to trade messages later tonight, and he's still planning to move here in April. Could it be this easy? Meet someone online that's actually cool instead of all the idiots I've met offline? Who knows, I guess we'll see, I should really clean my apartment and get some wine and peanut butter, but I also gotta figure out that daft playwright's schedule, why did I take him on as a client again? Oh well, it'll work out, or I'll make it work out, ha!

"Are you still there," I hear Mercury ask on the other end of the line. Shit, I forgot I was on the phone. I'm so bad at phones. I don't know why that is. Okay, cool, I'm still here.

"Yeah, just thinking about work stuff and Twitter boy."

"Cool, I can let you go."

"Alright, talk to you tomorrow."

"Yeah, I'll call you around seven or so," Mercury says. They always plan everything so well. I don't know how they do that. I look at my crime scene investigation of Ella's career on the wall, I guess we all have our little ways of managing the day-to-day life between the bigger events. That sounds like something Twitter boy would say, I think and laugh.

"I appreciate you," Mercury says in that soft, almost emotional voice, that comes out whenever they talk about anything that involves feelings.

"I love you too Mercury," I say and hear them say goodbye.

We get off the phone and I wonder if it really matters if I ever clean my apartment. I pull up Twitter again. Could it really be this easy after surviving all the assholes over the years, I wonder, maybe, I guess, stranger things have happened. Haven't they? I think they have. Yes, stranger things have happened, of course they have. Case says you just have to push through all the crap without losing yourself or your love for yourself and then someday you find something worthwhile. It sounds like more of the hippy crap they spout all the time, but who knows, maybe they're right. I'll ask them about it after I get some more wine and peanut butter, but I don't think I'll bother cleaning the apartment, I mean, who the hell cares anyway, right?

MERCURY

I was determined to be cool as I walked down North Broadway to meet up with Ella a week after the book signing in Pilsen that I almost went to before chickening out.

She told me just to meet her outside the Reckless Records. I was surprised when she texted me three days after the book signing. I felt a vicious urge to apologize for running away from our last meeting, but I held it in check. Her text said she was just checking in on me to make sure I was okay, and that she would love to grab coffee if I ever wanted to chat. I was thinking she thought I was an idiot, but I responded to the text anyway. I had this image of her laughing at me as she read my reply. I said I was okay. I said I had been thinking about what she said. I said we should probably hang out. I played it cool, I think. She said that would be fun and suggested meeting up in Boystown for coffee today. I half, well maybe a little more than half, expect her to tell me that our last meeting was actually a terrible joke.

"How you doing Mercury," I heard her ask before I spotted her in front of Reckless. I had been working so hard to look nonchalant that I wasn't looking up. I was looking down at my shorts, kind of surprised I could wear shorts in February in Chicago since I knew this was not normal weather for the city. I looked up and there she was in her own pair of shorts that I had to shake my head to stop staring at. She was dressed just as casually as I was, this made me feel good. This is no big deal, I told myself, I can handle this. Nothing's really going to ever happen between us after all, so there is nothing to worry about at all.

"Hi," I said and winced at the sound of my own voice. It seemed more nasally than usual to my ears, and I wondered if she noticed or if she saw me wince. Damnit! Why am I so nervous, nothing is going to happen! This is just a dream!

"Just so you know," she said smiling in a way that I swear was somehow sinister and sexy at the same time, "Linsk has cleared you so if we ever want to do anything or date or whatever, we can."

WHY THE HELL DID YOU JUST SAY THAT, I wanted to scream at her. I just stopped dead six feet from where she was standing. I swear I heard ominous music like the kind you hear in old horror movies start playing somewhere in the sky and slowly surround us. It got darker. I just know it did. Right then. The sun said forget this shit and went away. I thought I was going to pass out. It was the same feeling as her last bombshell about being attracted to me. I didn't know what to say. I didn't know what to think. What the hell was happening? It was like a Kacey Musgraves' song I heard months later, I was happy and sad at the same time. I wanted to both rip her clothes off and make the most passionate love of my life right there on Broadway in front of the record store and at the same time, run away so fast that Ella would suddenly realize that years ago I won competitions for my speed and skill in races throughout the area where I grew up. I wanted to grab her like a piece of candy given as a reward for a homework assignment and get away from her like a terrifying supernatural villain in the same horror movie that provided the damn music I swore was surrounding us from every direction.

"Are you okay," she said stepping toward me, only three feet between us now, as I felt myself sway on my feet. So much for playing it cool Mercury! I nodded and gave her one of what I always thought of as Christian side hugs – the kind where you limply touch the back of the other person with one arm as if you're not sure if you want to touch them or not. I knew I wanted to touch her. The feeling of her soft auburn hair brushing my shoulder during the side hug made me feel faint, but I also knew touching her felt very dangerous, like a door I wouldn't be able to close or a pathway into the forest where I could not plan my journey. "I'm sorry if I startled you," she said in what somehow seemed like the sexiest voice ever.

"I, uh, it's fine, I'm fine, how are you doing," there we go, I remembered how to talk. I can do this. I can play it cool. She rocked me there, why is her mouth so pretty? Why do I want to pick her up and swing her around like a teddy bear? Shit, calm down Mercury, you got this, it's fine. Shit! No, it's not fine, I only say that when I want a placeholder for saying something real, damnit, okay, calm down, it will be okay, I can do this. I took a deep breath that could have sent a sailboat off course, "It's fine, I was just surprised."

"I can understand that," she said shaking her head, "You want to grab a coffee, the Argo across the street has comfy seating." How does she seem so damn calm? What the hell is wrong with her? Doesn't she realize she just dropped another bomb on me out of nowhere?

"That sounds great," I said trying to make my face go neutral. I felt like I was grinning like an idiot and staring like a confused child lost in a department store when they suddenly find themselves in the toy section and could care less where or who they are anymore.

A few minutes later that felt like maybe a second and a half, damn time elasticity again, we were sitting in Argo. She was sipping her coffee. She didn't like the lack of outdoor seating in the winter. In Miami, she sat outdoors all year round. I was sipping my coffee. That's not true. I downed my coffee in almost only one sip like I usually do. I wondered if that seemed weird to her. Why am I so nervous? I stared across the table as she spoke. I watched her lips curl with every word, every syllable. I watched as her eyes seemed to become fields of light that pulled me in like the most addictive substance ever created. The way the light green and soft blue hues of the irises blended together seemed like a symbolic representation of the fluidity of nature. Oh great, I thought, I can think like the intelligent person I normally am, but I can't stop sounding like an idiot whenever I open my mouth, that's just great.

She explained the way her and Linsk and Reeves operated their relationship. I don't know if this was because I asked like I meant to or because she could just tell I was out of my depth at the moment. I was curious about nonmonogamy, but my own relationship history was an endless cycle of abuse, neglect, and being told how wrong and problematic I was. The way she openly talked about her feelings and relationship seemed so alien to me that I really did begin to wonder if she could generate a dragon from somewhere inside her head to come out and laugh at us while stealing our coffees. She talked about how they negotiate and share everything. How they have three rules – autonomy, egalitarianism, and never settle. She said she would like to get to know me because something about me seemed special or different from other people. I think I did actually faint for a second when she said that part. She said she would want to go slow, however, because she wasn't interested in any kind of hook up thing at this point in her life, she was only interested in deep, intimate friendships and partnerships.

I don't know if I said anything worth much of anything to her in response throughout this conversation. After what felt like five minutes, we both realized we had been at the Argo talking for five hours because it was somehow ten p.m. and the tea shop was closing. I didn't even notice how dark it had gotten or that it was colder than it was when we got here. As we got up from our seats, she asked if I wanted her to walk me to the train. I said yes. I almost told her that I get scared of walking alone at night, but I wasn't ready to share that yet. I think, maybe, she could tell because she asked if she could accompany me home and then made a point of saying she was happy to do so. I don't know why I said yes, nobody comes to my home, that's one of my rules, I have many rules, but I did say yes. She suggested we get a car instead of taking the train, and that was how we ended up outside my building at eleven o'clock at night on a Wednesday at the end of February 2018 smiling at each other as a cab drove away.

I don't know how I did it. Maybe my previous plan to play it cool was finally starting to work. Maybe I just had a moment of courage. I don't know, but I was standing there looking into her eyes wishing she would kiss me. I didn't know if she wanted to, and I wasn't sure I would not lose consciousness if she did, but I wanted her to kiss me right there in the kind of way you see in romantic comedies or music videos. I couldn't make myself kiss her, but in a moment of daring that still surprises me, I reached out and took her hand. The feel of her fingers intertwined with mine, wow, I felt like I was more alive than I had been before. It was like my veins became rivers and the blood within them was singing old love songs like the kind of thing I would expect to see in some cartoon movie. A few minutes or hours or whatever it was later, she told me she had a great time. She said we should do it again. She said she hoped I had sweet dreams. She hugged me soft and firm at the same time. She didn't kiss me, but I still felt somehow taller, stronger, and more, well, real as I entered my building.

ELLA

I felt like an idiot standing outside Reckless on North Broadway.

I texted Mercury a few days after my book signing in Pilsen. I just wanted to make sure they were okay after they didn't come to the signing. I was surprised they didn't come. I was pretty sure, as a result, that they were not happy with me. I couldn't blame them. They were probably working on a way to tell me they could never be attracted to me. I could see them running away from me on Michigan Avenue a couple weeks before. I didn't even know they could move that fast. I told them how I felt, but they looked at me like I said I was going to murder their childhood pets or something. I realized I didn't know if they had childhood pets. Mercury wasn't the type to reveal much about themselves. We had that in common, or well, a younger version of me had that in common with them. I didn't know if it was still the case. I was pretty sure they only agreed to meet me today to tell me nothing was going to happen.

I didn't like feeling so nervous. I wasn't used to it. The other times I had little friends, as I called them, during my time with Linsk and Reeves, it was always just a random kind of casual thing. I had not done anything like it in a little while because I felt so fulfilled that it seemed pointless to have little casual excursions. I could already tell that Linsk and Reeves were right, Mercury was no casual excursion. There was something special about them; something different, something I could only understand because of what Linsk, Reeves and the rest of our little family meant to me already. I thought about accidentally imagining them in the ninth seat at the big table in Pizano's. It seemed like such a silly fantasy as I stood outside the record store after arriving forty-five minutes early for some reason.

I spotted them before they saw me. This actually made me feel a little better. They were skipping and smiling. Maybe they were at least happy to see me. Maybe that meant I would still have my friend after they told me they were not attracted to me in any way. I took comfort in that possibility as I watched their body language change.

The skip became a walk. The smile became a soft, almost thoughtful, expression like someone looking over an old family gravestone on a rainy night in a black and white movie. I was thinking about Linsk telling me I should follow my feelings and see what happened. I was thinking about them saying this was good for me. I was thinking about the joy they had since we found Reeves that somehow only increased the joy we had together before and after the fact. I watched Mercury ducking their head as they got closer and closer to the record store. I tried to say something, but my voice caught in my throat.

I tried again. I failed again, story of my life. Finally, on the third try, I said, or I think I said, "How you doing Mercury," and thought, oh great, I don't just feel like an idiot, I sound like one too. They were cool as a cucumber when they looked up and saw me. I watched the buzz cut on top of their head because looking at them in a more direct manner felt way too hard, way too emotional for some reason. I could see the power, the muscled strength, in their perfect legs, and the way their torso blended with those glorious legs at the waist as if a master sculptor had figured out the perfect set of ingredients to drive me insane. I only ever knew one other being that could get this kind of reaction out of me, and that was the magical form of Linsk that I was still amazed I was lucky enough to wake up with and hold so many times.

"Hi," they said, and I immediately envied their poise and calm. Why couldn't I be that cool? How were they so calm? Maybe it was easier if you were the one in this interaction that wasn't interested or feeling anything.

I didn't want to learn that they were not interested yet so, with nothing else to say, I kind of just blurted out, "Just so you know," and tried but failed to make myself smile to hide just how terrified I felt, "Linsk has cleared you so if we ever want to do anything or date," why did I have to sound like such an idiot, "Or whatever," yeah, that's not any better Ella, "we can," I said and stopped myself from asking what they thought since I knew they would just tell me that they were not in any way interested in that type of thing.

It didn't matter. I could tell right away. They were not interested at all. I was so sure of it. They looked like they were about to throw up on the sidewalk. Even the thought of being anything other than platonic friends or acquaintances with me was enough to make them sick. I mentally tried to figure out just how fast I could run from them. I could tell from the last time we met that they could probably outrun me, but I didn't think they would bother chasing me down. If I ran away, I mean, they would have a much easier time. This is what I told myself. They wouldn't even have to let me down gently then. I was trying to remember just how far away the nearest train stop was from where we stood. The only thing that stopped me was the fact that I didn't want to be quite that much of an asshole or coward with someone that seemed like they really could be an amazing part of my life if they ever wanted to be in any form.

"Are you okay," I asked and hated the weak, desperate, and whiny sound of my own voice. "I'm sorry if I startled you," I said though I'm not sure if the words came out of my mouth in anything resembling a voice I could in any way be proud to possess.

"I'm fine," they said thankfully looking less sick than a moment ago, "How are you doing?" Well, I thought, there is your answer Ella. They just want to avoid the subject until they're ready to tell you they have no interest in you in any romantic way. An image of Linsk and Reeves taking care of me as I watched endless romantic comedies and Miranda Lambert music videos on our couch came scrolling through my mind. I wondered where the nearest ice cream place was, ice cream went well with being turned down, however gently, by someone you were just realizing was way too important to you already. I couldn't think of anything to say, but I began to breathe again as they added, "I'm fine, I was just surprised."

"I can understand that," I said, and then it was like time stopped. I don't really remember much after that moment. I know they asked about my relationship with Linsk and Reeves. I know that I responded by prattling on about it in likely the most boring way imaginable for what seemed like only a few minutes but must have been longer. I remember they seemed about as bored as I felt like they would be hanging out with me without a new novel or their school plans to talk about. Somehow, we ended up at the tea shop across the street. I remember I chose the spot in the first place because it was an area I felt very comfortable. I thought that would help the nerves. I was right and wrong at the same time. I remember I asked them how they were doing adjusting to Chicago. They said they were enjoying the city. They laughed and I felt like my heart would explode. I kept trying to stop myself, but I couldn't help it, I just stared into the depths of their brown eyes as they spoke wishing to drown in those swirling irises.

I remember we talked about the public health program they were starting in the fall. It was up at Northwestern. It was really exciting for them, and it reminded me of a lot of the work Linsk did. I remember that I had to go to the bathroom like three times and I thought they would think something was wrong with me. I remember that it seemed to take me forever to drink my coffee and I was sure they would think that was weird. I kept waiting for them to tell me they weren't interested, but it didn't happen. By the time I came back to my senses, or maybe the only parts my nerves allowed me to remember in full, the tea shop was closing. We had somehow spent the last five hours talking to each other. I had no clue how this happened. I remember thinking they seemed nervous when I mentioned walking them to the train.

I was pretty sure I imagined it, but it looked like they were scared. They were looking around as if the darkness was coming to get them. I offered, fairly sure they would turn me down and then finally tell me they weren't interested in anything romantic with me, to take them home. I was shocked when they said yes, and since the train question seemed to make them anxious, I suggested a car since I knew I could afford one even though they probably could not. They said yes again. I offered to pay for the car, so they could go alone, but they acted like they didn't even hear me. In the car, they kept saying something about rules that I didn't understand. When we got to their building, I realized it was a building that Case lived in at one point in the past. I also noticed that, to my surprise, they didn't go inside right away. We stood there staring at each other. I couldn't think of anything to say. I wanted to kiss them too much to think. I still had the image of them looking sick in my head, and for some reason, it seemed like they might faint right in front of me. From disgust or joy, my mind said, and though I was sure it was the former, I hoped it was the latter.

As I was thinking this, I suddenly had trouble breathing because they grabbed my hand. The touch of their skin felt like a lightning strike. It felt like the first time Linsk looked at me. It wasn't the same, after all they're not the same, but that was the closet comparison I had. I couldn't think. I couldn't talk. I remember them holding my hand. They actually smiled at me! I didn't know what to do. They said goodnight. I think I said something in response. I watched them walk into their building. I watched them get in the elevator. I stood there for, according to my phone when my brain finally started working again, for thirty minutes. I wanted to feel the touch of their skin again. I wanted to kiss them. I wanted to hope with all I had that they might somehow want these things too.

REEVES

If I'm being completely honest with you, I must admit that I was happier than I could have expected the night Ella came home from meeting Mercury at Reckless.

I did not plan to be visiting Chicago at the exact right time to greet Ella when she got home that night. I did not know that I would enjoy the experience so much ahead of time. I was just out in the living room grabbing a blanket because Linsk wanted to snuggle it after we made love just before Ella got home. I was getting used to the idea of Chicago. I was planning to get to know the city a little bit in the next few days. I knew Ella was out on what Linsk and I both thought of as a first date even though Ella didn't think she had a chance with Mercury. I knew that. I didn't know just how familiar the night would feel for me when Ella came in the apartment with a smile on her face twirling her auburn hair the way she does.

"Good night out with the next love of our lives," I said laughing and feeling the early onset of potential tears at the thought of what I said becoming reality. I have always been the most emotional one in the family, but at the moment, bursting into tears of joy about something Ella was so nervous about seemed funny to me.

"It was," Ella said softly in the voice that only seems to come out when she's very emotional even as she will say she is not emotional about anything ever, "Nice, I guess, I don't know what to make of it, I mean, they didn't say they weren't interested."

"Well," Linsk says coming out of the bedroom holding their Alice Cooper teddy bear and smiling at us, "What did they say?"

"I don't really remember much of what either of us said," Ella says laughing and we match her giggle for giggle. "It was kind of a blur, but they held my hand at the end."

Linsk gave Ella a hug and a kiss before taking the blanket from my arms, and saying, "Get your juicy muscles back to bed," to me, and "Unless you need us to process how you're feeling," to Ella.

"I'll be there in a minute," I said right as Ella said, "Nah, I think I want to process alone first if that makes any sense."

Linsk shook their little butt the cute way they do to make a point sometimes and laughed as they headed back into the master bedroom. I pulled Ella into one of my, what she calls, "how the hell do you do that bear hugs," and felt her breathe deeply against my chest. "Let us know if you need anything babe," I said before letting go of her and heading back to the bedroom to see what Linsk was up to with the blanket and the teddy bear. I could hear Ella moving out to the back porch, her spot as she would always say, as I climbed into bed. Linsk was cuddled up with the teddy bear, my childhood stuffed dinosaur, and the blanket on top of the sheets. I put my arms around them, soaking in the perfect mixture of their cologne and natural scent, kissed them on the head, and held their body tight still amazed by how wonderful our little family fit together.

I felt them slipping into dreamland, as Kaisa called it. My mind roamed back to the early days when these people first came into my life. I could see the look I had in my eyes back then in Ella's eyes tonight. I could hear the tremble in Linsk's voice back then in Ella's voice tonight. Linsk and I were right, the way Ella was right about us back then, this was something special. I didn't know what would happen, just like I didn't back then, but I knew, I could feel it, that this was important for Ella and the rest of the family. It was the same way that I felt like everything was more colorful, more natural, more alive when I met Linsk. It was that kind of feeling when I thought about Ella in the living room tonight.

I remembered when I left home after high school. I remembered how alone I felt in the world. I remembered the abuse, though for years I tried to block it out with substances. I remembered those days, it felt like just roaming through someone else's life, where it was more like a requirement to get up in the morning than a privilege or a gift. I touched the scars on my back with one of my hands. I heard that my, for lack of a better word, parents moved somewhere else a few years ago. I couldn't pretend to care that I didn't know where. I thought about these things in juxtaposition with the way Linsk felt in my arms. I thought about the way Ella dances around the kitchen when she has an especially fun story idea. I thought about the way Case loses their damn mind whenever a new Taylor Swift album comes out. I thought about the quiet patience Kaisa somehow brings to any problem any of us have. I thought about the sarcasm that starts dripping from the ceiling of any room where Linsk and Jo get together.

As Linsk's breathing got deeper and deeper and the sound of a Brandi Carlile album came in softly through the crack in the window from where Ella sat on the back porch probably reading the latest Bridget Jones style book she is in love with now, I smiled at the chance to meet with Michelle and Andrei tomorrow. I knew they had a whole day of "welcome to Chicago" planned for me, and since we had only gotten to hang out a few times when they visited Miami, I was really looking forward to feeling and becoming closer to them. I knew that Michelle and Linsk were going to work together on some healthcare initiatives. I knew that Andrei, through his work as a disc jockey, was planning to plug me in with other artists. I ran my finger down Linsk's spine softly and smiled at the possibilities that stretched out before our family as we continued to integrate into Chicago throughout the coming year.

CASE

I'm not, you should know, walking fast because I think I left the oven on, even though if that was the reason, it would be okay, it would be fine, it would be no problem.

But that is not what I am doing. I am walking fast because sometimes I walk fast. It has nothing to do with my anxiety. There are some things that have nothing to do with my anxiety. I'm sure there are. I was just sitting in Everybody's Coffee like I used to when I lived around the corner, and I finished the book I was reading. It was the kind I like most. The kind where Stephen King drives me crazy with something just creepy, scary, and whimsical enough to make my anxiety shut up for a few minutes, hours, days, or however long the novel will last. I'm not anxious at all right now. My speed down the sidewalk has nothing to do with the realization that I may have left the oven on when I left the house. It has nothing to do with that. If Kaisa texts me right now and says they are home and nothing is on fire, I will walk just as fast.

I say this, of course, right as Kaisa texts me saying they are home. I text back asking, just out of curiosity and not picking up speed at all if the house is okay. They text back saying it's not on fire and the door was locked and the windows were shut and the oven was not on and the cats are still alive and we didn't get robbed. They know me so well. I don't like to admit that I may have been incorrect because I feel myself walking slower without meaning to, but maybe it has to do with the fact that I recognize the shaved head and multicolored tank top ahead of me on this March afternoon, maybe that is why I'm slowing down, that could be it.

"Mercury," I say in the form of a question as I approach the familiar head and shirt from behind. We have only spoken a few times since they met Ella a couple years ago, but I know they are important to Ella, maybe even more so now, and to Jo who has become like a body part I cannot imagine making it through the week without at this point, so I should say hello. Yes, that is exactly what I should do. It's the polite thing and has nothing to do with feeling anxious. I did not, just so you know, think Mercury would hate me if they saw me on the street and I didn't say hello. I didn't think that at all. I also did not think that after this happened they would no longer like Ella and then it would be all my fault that Ella didn't get to fall in love with Mercury and dance in flowers or whatever the two of them might want to do together. I did not think that either. It is not a bad anxiety day, I just need to remind everyone of that right now.

"Oh," Mercury says, and I can hear the surprise in their voice, "Hey Case, what are you doing in this part of town?"

Oh shit, I surprised Mercury, but that's okay. It's fine. It is no problem. It's not like me surprising them is going to lead them to hate me now. No, that's not at all what I'm worrying about right now as I scratch the shit out of my arms and light my sixth cigarette in the two blocks from Everybody's Coffee, no, that's not it at all. And they're not going to run tell Ella that I'm an asshole who surprised them and get together with Ella and Jo on ways to remove me from their lives and, of course, take the cats and Kaisa and Linsk and Reeves and everyone else from me at the same time, that is SO not happening and I didn't even think of it. I'm fine, it's cool. They're not pissed at me, are they? I can't tell. Sirens show up somewhere in the distance, is Kaisa safe? Is Ella safe? Did the house catch on fire after all? Why are their sirens at this moment of all moments, "I used to live around the corner, what about you," I say to Mercury trying to figure out which direction the sirens are going in, not toward my house, I hope. Are they going toward my house? I text Kaisa.

"I live around the corner now," Mercury says laughing as Jo walks out of the shop on the corner across the street and Mercury and I both wave to her. About halfway across the street, Jo picks up her pace and when she gets to us she moves past Mercury in a swift motion and wraps her arms around me and starts rubbing my head the way Ella and Kaisa do.

"It's okay Case, it's okay, nobody hates you and everyone is safe, it's okay, we got you, you're here, you're safe, it's okay." As if they've known us forever, Mercury grabs me too and joins Jo telling me it's okay and holding me close. I feel myself shake in their arms. I can see it now. I can see the images of the gunshot going off, I can see the blood, I can feel the sound of the gunshot, I can feel it – I SCREAM, but not out loud. I'm shaking even more now and my phone goes off and Jo grabs it and tells me Kaisa is safe, it's okay, I can hear her now, Jo's face slides through the images of the gunshot, so does Mercury's face, I can see them, the faces are getting bigger, the gunshot is fading, I can breathe again, my chest shakes and I kind of collapse into their arms, "We got you Case, we got you, you're safe now," Jo says.

KAISA

"Thank you both for bringing them home," I say as I watch Case sleeping on the couch with Virginia, Lancelot, and Lux curled against them.

I think it's interesting that the cats can tell when Case has had an especially bad anxiety day or moment. They curl around them like a fortress. They don't move, like me I guess, until they are sure that Case is okay. I sometimes wonder if that kind of thing is part of the affinity I have always felt with cats. I remember that when I talked even less than I do now, they seemed to somehow still understand me, kind of like Ella does, without me having to say anything at all. Come to think of it, Ella is kind of like the unofficial, non-feline, family cat. She is where all our fears, worries, and other issues seem to go for comfort and care. I sometimes wonder if that is hard for her, but she says she loves being a caregiver, that it gives her meaning after such a terrible life. I guess I can understand that, I feel the same way about helping people through my work and I know the Linsk and Michelle share those same feelings.

"Are they going to be okay," Mercury asks in a soft whisper. This is my first time meeting them, but Linsk and Case both say Ella is in love with them. I can see why. There is something about them, the same kind of happy and sad after a life that has been harder than it should have been we all have. I can feel it in them. Ella and I both have that gift, like the cats.

"They will be more than okay," I say smiling, "This happens sometimes. They have a chronic anxiety condition, and some days are much, much worse than others. Like now, the trauma they experienced as a teenager comes roaring back to life inside their head and everything feels like it's falling apart. It is painful for them, and they will probably sleep for hours now that they are calm and home and safe, but they'll be great in a few hours and better than last time this happened because it's part of their healing."

The way Mercury nods says it all. They are one of us. There is something buried inside them. They have been through something, or multiple somethings, terrible. The nod says they understand. It's in their eyes as their head goes down and then back up – they know what Case is going through right now. Like the rest of us, Ella, Case and Linsk have found another big heart that has seen too much pain. I can see it already, they will become part of this family, whatever form their time with Ella takes, they fit here, they belong here. They don't know what that feels like yet, but they will. That's in their eyes too. They still think they need to be alone to survive. I remember that look, that false belief, that temporary survival mechanism.

Jo grabs Mercury's arm softly and nods. Mercury smiles, and because I remember just how scary the brain hidden behind that look can be, I reach out for them. We hug softly. I can tell they don't know what to think or feel about the sudden, from their perspective, embrace. I pat their head. I feel them shake the way we all do when crying, showing any emotion, is not something we feel safe enough to do yet, and I rub their head. I tell them thank you for taking care of my love and watch Jo smile at me with every ounce of light her face can carry. After our embrace, I walk Jo and Mercury to the door. Jo hugs me and says to call if I need her. I smile and say I will. I watch them leave, close the door, and go sit on the couch. I lift Case's head the way I always do and place it in my lap. I open my book, pet Lancelot, and sit with Case as they sleep. I'll be here with the cats, a fortress of love around them, when they wake up from this latest walk through the dark tunnels we all know so well.

LINSK

I can understand the birds hopping back and forth between the white lines of the road.

I am sitting on a bench that is kind of a chair outside a coffee shop. I was reading a nice novel about the ways health care experiences can shape personal identities. I was trading messages with Reeves on the phone in between sips of my tea and giggles at the sarcastic commentary of the narrator. I was thinking about Ella coming home last night telling me she kissed Mercury and to her surprise, the world did not explode. I was enjoying the feeling of the sunshine as it kissed the edges of my face above the silk scarf I wrapped around my neck as I left the office an hour ago. I was remembering when Ella showed up with the scarf after she went roaming around some place called Apalachicola looking for story ideas sometime last year. Reeves was saying he found a new idea for a way to paint algae on the messenger app on my phone. I was absentmindedly rubbing my leg because it was still a little sore from a tough morning where my bladder seemed to be trying to convince me of the benefits of suicide. I was doing all of these things without thinking much of them when I saw the birds.

The first bird came out of the sky and landed in the middle of the white line. It is the kind of white line that separates a turning lane from a regular lane on yet another road. There was a piece of toast or maybe biscuit on the white line that someone had discarded when walking to the series of cafes I sit in front of or driving by in a hurry to some other equally anonymous setting in the city. The bird swooped down to check it out. It started pecking at the food. It would hop up into the air when the next car came and the next and the next after that. It was joined by another bird. This one was red, the first one was black. They danced, in a way, up into the air and back to the toast on the ground, somehow always missing the cars coming. It was like they were used to the interruption, and just learned how to work around it. They didn't seem to mind, but I wondered if it was much harder for them than it looked from a distance.

I could relate. I was feeling the same way as I felt the latest stinging pain rip through my abdomen. I know no one could tell. The man sitting in front of me with his *Chicago Tribune* didn't even look up. The woman sitting at the table next to me with her Meg Donohue novel smiled at me, which makes me think I may have smiled to cover the pain. Or maybe she just smiles when something draws her from the book at a busy café. I wonder if people can feel it when something shifts, like the position of the knife-like pain in my abdomen, in the vicinity of wherever they are continuing their isolated lives at a given moment. A young white woman with pig tails swings by on a skateboard singing a Demi Lovato song at the top of her lungs. She might be eleven or maybe eighteen or maybe ageless in the way young people showing no pain seem to those of us who've managed to live a little longer despite our pain.

The pain has become a low hum. The birds are still enjoying their lunch-dance as I now think of it. The cars interrupt their natural rhythm the way the pain interrupts my day. I was going to go shopping. I was going to check out this vegetable stand type market Kaisa told me about. I didn't know it was going to be a bad day, but I guess those are the days I never see coming and even now that I have less of them, they still shock me to the core and sap all the energy out of me in ways that make me want to scream. Screaming is not appropriate, however, when sitting in my office trying to help other people with their own pain. I also don't like others to see me struggle. Ella can see, Case and Reeves and Kaisa too if it's really bad, but mostly I like to take care of myself. Autoimmune, that's the word that has followed me since I was a small child. Autoimmune, that's the soundtrack to throwing up, sweaty nights when I'm so cold I swear I'm in a blizzard. Autoimmune, that's the best answer they can give me in the white coats and sterile rooms. Autoimmune, that's what my tears spell when it hurts too much to do anything.

The birds finish their lunch. They head east in the sky and I wonder if they're laughing or complaining about the interruptions of the cars. I head west on foot wondering if the market is still open and why it seems like everywhere in the Midwest, even in the heart of the city, closes so early. My phone vibrates again. Reeves is mixing paints.

I ask him if he's ever considered a series of paintings or maybe just one on the lunching habits of birds in cities. I pass the youthful singer with the skateboard on the next block. She is pulling on her pigtails and staring at a street sign. I wonder if she is lost. A bird sits down on the sidewalk beside her. I wonder if it is lost. Maybe we're all just looking for the next interruption in the series of events that make up our lives.

JO

"I need some sexy time music," I say to Case as we flip through records at Dave's on a windy afternoon.

Mercury is looking at Brandy Carlile albums. Case is searching for a Taylor Swift record they don't have, which is funny because they always do this even though there is not a Taylor Swift record they don't have until she releases another one. It soothes them, they say. I asked a few trips ago when we were at another record store. Case wasn't all that into record stores and even music, beyond the obvious pop stuff we both heard growing up with all the other white kids in the suburbs, until they came to Chicago. They told me how they adopted Ella's habit of going to record stores when they felt off or anxious more so than usual. They would just look for something even if they knew it didn't exist. They said the looking was a way to relax. It gave you something to focus on. It was a search, but the outcome wasn't the point.

"What kind of music is sexy time music for you," Mercury said from across the shop.

"I don't know, not sure I even remember what sexy time is for me," I say laughing and flipping my hair as Mercury moves to the bin marked with an S. I'm kind of joking, but I'm kind of not joking.

"I like St. Vincent and other kinds of electro pop for that kind of stuff," Case says blushing the way they always do when sex comes up in conversation.

"I don't usually play music when," Mercury starts to say then stops. "Is this about Twitter boy?"

"Yes," I say, "I'm planning way in advance, kind of dreaming into the future," I say laughing again and again only kind of half joking at best. I keep trading messages with this guy on Twitter. He's so funny, but more so, he seems like the opposite of the assholes and idiots I've managed to attract before, "I usually use some random dance or hip hop music, but I don't know, I feel like Twitter boy might be worth actually picking out some music."

I make my way down the aisle. I guess I would call it an aisle. It's Dave's so there isn't much room. There are just two tight rows of records. I pick up an Usher album. "Not that one," Mercury says, "That's not his sexy time album."

"Do you have any of the singles Death Cab for Cutie put out a while back," I hear Case ask the guy behind the counter who is probably Dave or someone we all think is Dave because we never ask, but he is always here. He says something in reply.

"I always liked this one a lot and I don't have it on vinyl," I say to Mercury still looking over the Usher album.

"What," Mercury says running their hand through the buzz cut that fits their face as if a painter picked it out for them at a moment where their most important portrait was about to be painted for royalty of a bygone era. "I don't think that one is that good."

"Whatever," I say laughing and watching the horrified look on Mercury's face. I like this look, it's a fun one. Case is digging through the boxes of vinyl singles that Dave or the guy who looks like maybe he is Dave or whoever arranges the place always has on the front far left of the counter. They knew the singles would be there. They also know they have all the singles. They also know that Dave only has one of them as of the last time we were in the shop.

Mercury starts to defend their opinion of this Usher album, but I say, "So, how do you feel about kissing Ella?"

I watch their face become a synonym for tomato and Case joins us with a smile saying, "Yeah, how are you feeling about that?"

"I, uh, um," the red of their face reminds me of the sight of a stop sign caught just so in the sunshine on a summer day, "It was, well, I guess, it's fine, it's good." They kind of bury their face in the Billy Moon t-shirt they like to wear on days where they're feeling more relaxed, comfortable, and confident. They are trying to hide. I could give them hell for a while, but I'm in a good mood and my phone tells me I have a new message from Twitter boy.

"Okay," I say putting my arm around their shoulders, "I'll leave you alone, let's go get some donuts."

Case nods and falls in with us as we leave Dave's without having found anything to buy today. I smile at Mercury as they continue to model the latest in blush aesthetic. They were talking about the kiss when I picked them up this morning. Last night, they met up with Ella for the second meeting or date since they found out Ella was attracted to them. They went walking along the lake near where Mercury lives. They were holding hands. There was a cute puppy walking by with its owner or parent or whatever smiling at everything in sight. Ella told Mercury that she wanted to kiss them. That is so Ella, I thought as Mercury relayed the story. Mercury told Ella they wanted that too. Mercury said they were about to fall down so they sat on a bench. Ella sat with them. She grabbed Mercury's hand. "It felt like I was dreaming," Mercury said.

We move up the block from Dave's heading for Stan's Donuts. It's my favorite and Case's favorite too because of Ella. She is addicted to the place. Every time she visited us in the city she just had to go there, this one and the one in Wicker Park and the one at the Roosevelt stop, like twenty times. We would sit in one of the Stan's and talk shit about our lives. Ella would eat these nasty Captain Crunch donuts she said were the best thing ever. Case would get these huge, and tantalizing, I admit, peanut butter and chocolate things that made so much of a mess that you just knew they were amazing because otherwise no one would put up with the mess. I would vary what I got, never able to make a decision, donuts or lovers, I just never know what I want. We enter the donut shop, and Case runs up to the counter to see if they have the peanut butter things and maybe one of the gluten-free donuts to take to Kaisa.

Mercury was quiet on the walk from Dave's. They're trying to make sense of Ella. Good luck with that, I want to say. Ella is just Ella, figuring her out is like trying to understand a puzzle with only about one percent of the pieces. That seems like something I could put on Twitter. Twitter Boy would love it. Mercury said they felt, "Like I was in deep trouble," when Ella kissed them, and even more so, when the kissing continued beyond the first touch of the lips. I know what they mean. I like Twitter boy way more than I'm comfortable with. I know Mercury thinks this is a fling or just a little nothing to Ella, but again, Ella is a bit different from anyone else, so I bet Mercury is in for a surprise. Plus, though they haven't told Mercury, Case thinks Ella is actually in love with Mercury and Case says Linsk thinks the same.

I wonder what will happen with them and with Twitter boy as I try once again to figure out the difference between a coffee roll and a donut. This is the kind of thing that drives me crazy. I don't know what the difference is, and I bet it doesn't matter, but I still really want to know. Case gets the peanut butter thing, and just for fun, I order one of the damn Captain Crunch things Ella. Mercury gets a small coffee with two Splenda and some cream, but no donuts. My phone vibrates again. I should get better at ignoring it, better at checking it, or maybe both. I take a bite of the donut that Ella loves, and I again try to figure out what is so special about it, maybe I'll never know.

CASE

"So Linsk says you're in love with Mercury, you okay with that yet," I say to Ella as Linsk belts out the latest amazing notes from the Cranberries song they are singing at this southside karaoke bar Reeves found while he was hanging out with Andrei.

"As scary as it sounds, I think Linsk is right about this," Ella says smiling at Linsk as they hit the final note in the song. There is always a kind of glow in Ella's eyes when she watches Linsk perform. She will gush about waking up to Linsk strumming and singing Wilco's "Jesus Etc." in the mornings. She has that look right now as she says, "I'm not sure if I'm okay with it yet, I mean we've only hung out a few times, but there is something, what did you and Reeves say, special, here, I think."

The crowd goes nuts the same way they do every time Linsk performs anywhere for a public audience. I try to visualize young Linsk in theater productions and playing various characters. I see them dancing with their head bobbing the way they do at the goth clubs while Ella stands to the side of the dance floor smiling at them. I see them head banging to this or that metal band at hole-in-the-wall clubs all over the south. They bow. People scream more. They acquiesce. A song by the Cure that means a lot to them and Reeves begins. The crowd gets into it. Linsk is egging them on the way the few people with magical performance skills seem to be able to do. They start singing and it's like a trance covers the room the way rain can cover a sidewalk that seemed so ordinary a moment before.

"Well," I say taking a sip of a Rekorderlig Cider, "Just follow your feelings is what you're always telling the rest of us."

"Yeah," she says smiling, "Let's grab a smoke."

We move to the outside of the building. I can hear Linsk hitting the chorus hard in the background. We pass Andrei and Ella stops to give him a hug. He's hanging out with some of his buddies who do gigs in the area and talking to some white woman with pink hair and an Elvis Costello shirt. She is saying something about Russian cuisine, and he is trying to explain something about spices used in some dish from where his grandmother grew up long ago. I give him a side hug and wonder what Michelle is up to down in Texas. She's visiting her father as he moves to the next transitional housing in his ongoing battle with his health. Years ago, I remember wondering if Ella and Michelle would make a cute couple, and I smile at the memory as we reach the outside and Ella lights a smoke.

"It was magical, kissing them, each time, but especially that first time over by the lake, it was the same thing holding their hand for the first time." I remember Ella saying how the two of them kept lightly, accidentally Ella said, touching each other's hands in the back of the car on the way to Mercury's building. I remember Ella saying that Mercury finally whispered, "You can hold my hand, if you want," and she felt this immediate urgency to grab Mercury's hand and maybe never let go for even a second. I remember even further back to when Ella had similar overwhelming moments with Linsk that predicted just how close they would become and remain. I remember a time between these points when Reeves and Linsk expressed similar overwhelming experiences with each other that would build and grow over time. I remember around the same time as Reeves and Linsk were coming together feeling the shock through my system at the simple, soft feel of Kaisa's fingers in my hair, against my shoulder, and against my cheek on a Chicago Street.

"Well, I was actually with Mercury and Jo earlier today, and I think they're pretty damn into you too so maybe all this, what did you call it, emo stuff," Ella nods and takes a drag off her Camel, "Maybe it's like the other times we've all found something special."

I take another drag off my cigarette as Ella says, "Maybe, I guess I hope so, but I think I forgot how scary it was to feel so much in those moments advising you and Linsk when it came to Kaisa and Reeves." She smiles and giggles a little bit in the way she does when Linsk tickles her. She shakes her head and for just a moment, she looks about as red in the face as Mercury was earlier when Jo asked about the two of them kissing the other night. She throws out her cigarette, and I do the same. We head back inside and find Linsk sitting at the table the three of us have been parked at for a few hours now. People come by and compliment Linsk on their singing, and in between these compliments, Ella leans down and gives them a soft kiss. Both of them somehow glow. They say Kaisa and I do too. I wonder if it's some kind of external sign of intimacy like Spanish Moss starting to sway in a different direction just before a storm hits the shores of south Florida.

MERCURY

I don't believe in fate, deities, or any of that other crap, but sometimes I have to wonder.

I shot up in bed with sweat dripping from my body. I could still feel the cold air of the deserted highway in 2016. I can still hear and somehow feel the sirens. I am naked. My clothes somewhere on the floor, I'm guessing. My novel is missing too. Where is my phone? I feel the grips of panic running through me. I can see her. I can almost feel her. I can almost touch her. I beg my mind to shut down. I beg her to leave my thoughts. I beg the world to dissolve into nothing. I want to vomit. I have to get her out of me somehow. I need to vomit. I stumble trying to get out of the bed. It's a damn piece of shit, like everything else in this apartment, like everything else inside me. I fall to my knees on the soft though hard surface of the floor. I want to scream. I need to throw up. I want a drink, a big drink with enough alcohol to wipe her away for good. I start to tremble. I want to cry. Why can't I cry? Why is my body so hot? My knees hurt. I stand, wobble, I move toward the bathroom, why isn't it closer?

I hear my phone go off. Who the hell is awake this late? It's the middle of the night. I keep moving to the bathroom. My phone is on the floor in the hallway between the living area and the bathroom. How did it get there? I want to ignore it. I need to throw up. I can still see her. She's there in my eyes the same way my phone is there in my eyes. I should ignore the phone. I should get to the bathroom. I need something I can control! I stop. I pick up the phone. It is a text message. It is from Ella. It says, "Hey beautiful, I miss you, wanna get together sometime tomorrow?" I stare at it. I don't even notice as my legs go out from under me.

I'm transported back to Agnes Scott College in 2016. The day is as dark and terrible as any other in history. I can't breathe. I see her everywhere. I just want to die. I always want to die ever since that night on the highway. I can hear the sirens. I can feel her. I can, I can't, I can't, I turn quick around the building that I was about to throw up on and see a crowd of people. There is something going on. I don't know what. I see Jo in the front row. I take a seat in the back. There is a woman talking about pain. She has what looks like the softest auburn hair I've ever seen. She is smiling and gesturing with her right hand as she talks about some story. It is her story. Well, not her story, I guess, it's a story she wrote. She talks about writing as a way to manage the pain, as a way to heal from what we can't control, what we can't make sense of in any other way. I sit in the back row transfixed. She is wearing a pink head band. She is talking about what it was like growing up as someone people expected to be a boy. She talks about being beaten, raped, and abused by people when she was, I realize in a moment of overwhelming emotion, about my age. I can see the unshed tears in her eyes. They match the ones that start running down my own face in the back row of the auditorium.

I don't even know how I got here, I think sitting cross legged on the floor of the hallway in my apartment between the bathroom and the living area. I'm holding my phone so tight that I'm surprised it doesn't break. Later, it will have issues charging and I will wonder if I did that in the midst of one of these nightmare-filled nights sitting on the floor. I'm staring at the text message. I don't know how many times I read it. I wonder if it's a joke. I wonder if it's a booty call. I wonder what game Ella is playing with me. She writes thrillers, after all. Maybe she is teasing me to come up with story ideas. I can't imagine that she might actually like me. I remember the softness of her lips on mine. I could hear the lake. It was singing a love song as our lips pressed together, the kind of song Sara Bareilles would sing, the kind with a soft sweeping piano in the middle of it. I can feel her in the apartment with me somehow. I can feel the way her auburn locks shimmer against my fingertips. Why am I naked?

I remember standing in the back of the auditorium while Jo and the others in line went up, one by one, to talk to Ella and get their novels signed. I was just standing there. I wanted to be close to her. I wanted to run away from her as fast as I could. I wanted to know what the hell to do. Jo came bouncing up the stairs after spotting me standing in the back. The line was dying down a bit. Jo hugged me. She giggled and showed me the book. She asked if I was going to go up and meet the author. The author, that was all we knew to call Ella then. I shook my head. I couldn't really talk. I remember that Ella was wearing a white skirt and a band t-shirt. I didn't know the band at the time. I looked them up that night in my room. It was a band called Wilco. I remember that Jo said I should say hello. I said I didn't have a book. It was all I could say. Jo said it wouldn't matter, I should say hello. I said I don't know how.

I text Ella back. I don't know how long it took me. I wonder if she's making fun of me by calling me beautiful. I send the text anyway. It says, "I could probably get together tomorrow." It's cool, calm, I don't want to sound needy. That's what everyone else has always said I am, well, everyone but Jo. And…but I don't want to think about her now, I push the memory away. I get up off the floor. My clothes are near the bed. I don't want to wear them. It's like they're stained by whatever woke me up. I pull out a tank top that feels good against my skin. I put on a pair of shorts. They are the same shorts Ella said looked cute on me when we met up for coffee one time when we were both in Nashville for work. They are the same shorts I wore on our first meeting after they said they were attracted to me. They are the same shorts I was wearing when Ella held my hand after I said she could. I sit on my piece of shit couch. I'm not ready to get in bed. I wonder if she'll text me back soon.

I walked down the steps of the auditorium. I was holding Jo's hand. She was leading me. I marveled at her confidence. She walked right up to the author, Ella, and said my name and that I wanted to say hello. I blushed. Ella turned to me. It was like she looked right through me. It was like all my masks went on vacation at the same time. I once saw a kid who looked lonely or maybe just tired receive a stuffed Disney animal in a parking lot and burst into tears and grins like his heart had been opened out of nowhere. I felt like that. It was like she could see into my soul if I have such a thing. It was like she could read me like a book. I didn't like the feeling. I felt exposed. I liked the feeling. I felt real. It was an odd juxtaposition that I spent weeks trying to put into words.

Ella texts me back about the same time I get into bed. She says, "Well, if you can't get together, no worries, but how about I text you tomorrow afternoon to see what you're up to?"

I wait five minutes. I don't want to seem too eager. That is what other people told me was a bad thing, one of the many bad things about me everyone has taught me over the years. I texted back, after six minutes just in case, "That sounds cool."

"Great," she texts back right away, which strikes me as strange, "Goodnight Mercury."

I want to text her back, but I don't. I just sit there watching the screen. I know I fall asleep at some point, but all I remember is reading and re-reading her text and hoping she would text me the next day.

ANDREI

The bar is almost empty as Ella and Linsk kiss under the pseudo moonlight provided by the street lamp.

Linsk and Case head for the car Linsk called because they need to get home. Linsk has plans to fly down to see Reeves in the morning. Case has to get home because they have to be up early to do something at the university they work at, maybe interview someone, I can't recall. Ella and I head out of No. 18 Karaoke Bar toward the Cermak-Chinatown Red Line station. Ella wants coffee and I want to roam so we're headed to the 24-hour Dunkin' Donuts in the Loop. Ella is humming a song that I can't quite place while swinging her hair from side to side. Michelle got to Texas safely, and the cats are good so no need to go home in any hurry.

"What are you humming," I ask as we get on the red line.

"Some Taylor Swift song, I think it's from the *1989* album, or maybe its older, it's about starting over in a new relationship."

"Mercury on your mind dear," I say smiling and chuckling. Linsk closed their standing-ovation-as-always performance of the night with a Taylor Swift song about being in the woods or done with the woods or something like that. They were winking at Ella when they were singing the song. It was such a great example of trolling someone without being too obvious about it. That is, after all, a skill Linsk has in spades. I remember when Reeves was in town they had me do a Lisa Loeb song just for him, and to make him blush, when we were at the karaoke bar near the loop, what is it, oh yeah, Brando's. Reeves was giggling the whole time because he apparently has a not-so-secret love affair with Loeb. If I'm being completely honest with you, I really enjoy playing along with each and every way Linsk comes up with to troll the people they love, and in fact, I probably love it more than is healthy.

Laughing, Ella says, "Yeah, I guess so, seems like they're starting to take up residence in my head."

"So, shoot them a text, maybe they're out and about."

"I don't want to wake them up, I mean, it is after two in the morning and they seem like more of a morning person," Ella says smiling and blushing at the same time.

We get off at the Monroe station, and head for the Dunkin' Donuts we went to the first time the two of us hung out while Linsk was up here for a conference. They were staying at the Palmer House and Michelle had been saying for over a year that Ella and I would so be best friends if we spent some time together. She was right. She usually is. Linsk also really liked having me along because, as they told me later, Ella is often automatically scared of men after all she's been through, so it was good for her to have another man, other than Reeves, who she could feel safe and comfortable around. I still feel honored to provide this service.

"Just text them, if you wake them up, apologize."

We order our coffees, give the homeless man outside the Dunkin' a coffee and some bills to get some food, drugs, alcohol, or whatever might help him survive another night. Who cares what he buys, Linsk and my grandmother would say, he needs help we can provide so we should do it, simple as that. After debating it from every angle throughout our time walking to, through, and out of the donut shop, Ella finally agrees with me and sends Mercury a text. I watch her smoking her cigarette against a pole near the Monroe Blue Line station a few minutes later. She is swinging her hair around her shoulders, and I remember commenting on the sweet auburn of her hair in a picture Michelle had back when Michelle thought Ella and I would make a cute couple before we had ever met. I miss Michelle. I hope Texas goes well. There is a sense you get for someone, having them nearby, after years together, I feel it whenever she goes away for work or some other reason and like tonight, I take longer to get home when she's not there.

Ella plays with her phone throughout the ride to Logan Square. We both live in the neighborhood now, and Ella often sits out on our back porch with Michelle and I talking shit about this or that musician or novelist. Michelle will be sipping champagne and laughing. I will be smoking a joint and asking Ella's thoughts on whatever book I'm reading. Ella will be sipping whatever champagne Michelle likes that week and trying to understand everything about whatever plants I'm growing at the time or my work mixing songs and soundbites in clubs and for advertising firms. Michelle will bring up her work, and Ella and I will flood the porch with questions about this or that major health issue she's working on at a given time. I watch Ella playing on her phone, both of us go silent for long periods, it fits us.

"You okay," I say as we leave the Logan Square station.

"I guess," she says looking at me, "Mercury doesn't seem all that interested, but I guess I'll text back tomorrow to see if they're free."

"Maybe they're just playing it cool," I say.

"You know I have no clue what that means."

"And that is part of what makes you adorable to the rest of us," I say as we take the familiar right on Troy Street heading to our respective homes for the night.

JO

"Why are we meeting here," I ask Case as they come bouncing up to me in front of the Lids on State Street.

"I don't know," Case says smiling and giving me a hug, "This is where Ella said to meet." Case is wearing one of their favorite outfits, and I smile because I always love the sight of them in their oversized shorts, baggy flannel shirt, and knock-off Doc Martens. There is something about this look that really seems to both fit them as a person and accentuate the body art – especially the cello on their right shoulder – adorning the uncovered skin. As we hug, I smell the familiar scent, the I haven't bathed all that much lately smell, that seems to follow Case around many of the days of the year and especially in the winter.

"What's she up to this time?" Case releases my body. I check my phone. Twitter boy has been quiet today both with me and on Twitter itself. I started tweeting more lately, I think that's how you say it. I am enjoying it. I don't know if I'm any good at it, but I know I will be. I wonder what Twitter boy is up to. I wonder if he's staring out some window in his city thinking of the next funnier-than-it-should-be thing he will post online. I hope so.

"No clue," Case lights a cigarette and runs a finger through their short, close-cropped brown hair, "She just said to meet her here," Case looks at their phone, "About five minutes ago." The smoke from the cigarette dances on the wind, the kind of wind that I used to think people were referring to when they called Chicago the windy city, but of course, now I know the real story behind the nickname and I admit I like the actual story better after all. I watch the smoke leave us behind in its journey to wherever smoke goes after we lose sight of it. This is the kind of thing I can wonder about all night, where, in fact, does the smoke go?

"Then where is she," I say right as I spot her coming around the corner. It looks like she's coming from the Palmer House, which makes me think she went to the little café and bakery she likes next door to it. I can't tell from here if the cup she's holding is one of theirs, but I'm pretty sure it is. We are standing in front of Lids, and I'm trying to remember the last time I was in the loop for anything other than changing trains, Pizzano's Pizza, or going to the park. I can't remember. It's funny. This may be the part of Chicago most well known outside the city, but most of the time, I never come anywhere near here and I know that's true for Case as well. I watch the people walking in varied directions across the street. I wonder if any of them are having any fun or if maybe they're all just trying to find some fun somewhere.

"Good evening beautiful people," Ella says arriving in front of the two of us in front of the chain store that I've never been inside despite walking past it a few times. Her hair is swaying in the breeze, which creates a shimmering effect since both the light blue t-shirt and the soft, off-white skirt she wears this night are also shimmering at the same pace and speed as her hair. She hugs us both flipping her left foot back on each embrace. "So, I know this sounds silly, but I was thinking that since the three of us keep spending more and more time together, we should have our own kind of shared thing, if you'll forgive the annoying writer just a smidge of sentimental symbolism or at least keep your complaints for the ears of others."

Case and I both giggle. These are the kinds of things that only Ella ever seems to say. It's one of the more fun things about her, this, as Linsk puts it, "childlike whimsy" that captivates and confuses in equal parts. I nod giving her the look I give her that she says reminds her of "a teacher I had years ago that was always mad at me for some reason I never understood, and yet also gave me free books and candy when no one was looking." Case calls it my "mischievous look," like I'm up to no good but something, hell, everything at the same time. "What do you have in mind," I say to Ella as she smiles at the entry to Lids.

"Well," she says, "I feel like it must be sad to be celebrating losing every day throughout the spring and summer, so I thought you and I would keep Case company this year."

I start laughing right as Case says, "Whatever Ella, maybe they'll be good this year."

"And maybe I'll go tap dancing in the garden on top of the Palmer House with a unicorn named Frank and an endless supply of taffy, but I'm not betting on it."

Case makes their own "I'm-looking-annoyed-but-I'm-not-really-annoyed face" as Ella opens the door and the three of us go inside. "So, what, you're going to cheer for the Sox with me this year?"

"Not exactly," Ella says sticking her tongue out and passing a black Chicago White Sox baseball cap to Case, "I'm going to get us all Sox hats, so we can laugh at you cheering for the Sox this year in style." Case tries on the hat and grins. Ella throws one to me as well and picks out a burgundy one for herself. Case and I both have black ones, but Ella always has to be different in some way, it's kind of her thing. We each try on about three hundred other hats even though the store obviously doesn't have quite that many to choose from, but in the end, we each pick out and leave wearing the one's Ella picked up in the first place. Together, we exit the store advertising the baseball team that captured Case's heart the previous summer and laughing about the fact that neither Ella nor I actually follow baseball at all. Ella says, "Well, that's what really makes these the perfect matching accessories for us, no one would see it coming."

Outside lighting another smoke beneath the brim of their new, jet-black, baseball cap with SOX on the front of it, Case says, "So, honey, was the whole point of tonight just to come give me hell and get yourself a hat to wear when the wind makes that long hair annoying?"

Turning to me, Ella says, "Why do they think tonight needs to have a point?"

"Beats me," I say laughing and putting my arm around Ella's waist. Together, we start skipping down State Street with Case coming up, at first, behind us, and then, right beside us. Laughing, I say, "I do know where we're headed next since there doesn't seem to be any real purpose to this particular meet up in the middle of the city."

"Do tell sweet Jo," Ella says laughing, lighting her own smoke, and shaking the ponytail she fashioned in the Lids by putting her hair through the hole in the back of her new burgundy White Sox hat. She shakes it a couple more times and blows smoke at Case. Case laughs. My phone buzzes and Twitter boy informs me that he misses me. I blush, I feel it on my cheeks. Before I can say anything, Ella says, "Must be Twitter boy," and her and Case lock arms and start skipping down the sidewalk screaming, "First comes love, then comes marriage…"

As we turn left onto Lake Street, I say, "I knew it," and both of them nod as we head for the Jason's Deli that Ella used to always take us to when she was visiting.

LINSK

There is a smile written in the shadows of the bedroom tonight.

I feel Ella breathing. Her face rests on my stomach, what little stomach I have. The night outside is quieter than it should be on a weekend. There are no sounds surrounding the apartment, just space and calm. I run my fingers through the auburn sections of Ella's hair. I remember her recently learning that she had what people call an hombre. Her hair does it naturally, shades of auburn, red, brown, and blonde bounce against and buffer each other as the hair flows down her back. Someone asked her where she got her hair done. She said she didn't have a place in Chicago yet. The person seemed confused. Ella was confused. Mercury explained that people paid a lot of money for hair like hers. Ella asked me about it. I confirmed what Mercury said. Ella was mystified since she doesn't even own a brush.

I feel Ella wiggle her butt against my body. Reeves does this too when he's asleep and I'm sitting up watching him breathe. It is a beautiful feeling. It is like so many things, small, not necessarily noticed beyond the confines of a private moment, but priceless and shared at the same time. I remember holding Ella as she cried in my arms the first time. We were so much younger, it seems, but we felt so old, like trees battered by storms, we were holding on with all we had, but our roots were straining until we found each other. We were making love. She started to shudder. She started to shake. The tears came out of nowhere. She was crying. I was holding her. It was on a futon that was cheaper than a clearance rack. It was in an apartment that was in a former hotel that was so badly maintained that I often wondered if the floor would fall in on us one of those nights. It was in 2011. We were new to each other then.

Back here, in this room in Logan Square, in 2018, I feel her shake in her sleep. She doesn't do that as much as she used to. I don't either. There were times when I was like a theatre production blending high comedy and drama in my own sleep. That was also years ago. We were new then too. Back then, I remember wondering how long I might get to hold Ella. These days, I know, somehow, that the answer to that is infinite, and yet, it still feels just as fresh, just as important, just as urgent as when we were younger, when we were new. Maybe that's what intimacy does, I wrote in a notebook no one ever got to read, maybe it lets you feel the utter power of the first time over and over again for an infinite period of time. I remember Ella giving me a book of poems she wrote for me last year. I remember sharing my own poems with her over the years. What if life is poetry, she once asked me, I like to think it is, I responded.

I should be sleeping. I have work in the morning. Reeves is coming in for a visit at the end of the week. Springtime has arrived in the city. March is marching on its merry way. I should be sleeping. Instead, I brush Ella's hair watching the shadows on the wall form shapes for my eyes, and my eyes only, to devour. There is a smile. There is a rainbow. There is a subway or maybe it's a highway. There is something in the shadows that wasn't always there, peace. I used to look in the shadows and worry about being swallowed, lost, left out of something, taken away. I used to avoid them. Now, I smile at the shadows, an interpretive exercise if there ever was one. I feel my eyes getting heavy. Ella stirs in my arms and I rub the edge of her shoulder blade. I smile at the feeling of her skin in my hands, my long fingers finding her spaces, her curves, her dimensions. I kiss her softly on her head as my eyes begin to close.

ELLA

Linsk swims in the blanket draped over them.

Slowly, careful not to wake them, I pick them up. I carry them the dozens of steps to the master bedroom. The apartment in Logan has three bedrooms. It costs a fortune. We needed a bedroom for any of us to use as an individual space, especially once Reeves arrives. We needed a bedroom Linsk could use as an office. And then, we have a master bedroom with the bamboo bed we share with each other some nights, the same way they share it with Reeves some nights, the same way the three of us sleep there other nights. I can feel them breathing in my arms. It is a Monday night in late March. I was out in Wicker Park getting ice cream with Mercury. I came home to find the Netflix on a screen saver, and Linsk out cold on the couch. They look and feel so peaceful. I place them in our bed, wrap them in covers, and position myself behind them.

I run my hands softly through their hair, and smile at the way their body fits perfectly into the crook of my arm. I remember the first time I held them like this. It was in a nice apartment, not like the shitty one I had near campus that used to be a hotel, a few miles from the University of Miami. They fell asleep on the couch watching *Breaking Bad*. Same couch, different apartment, different city, this was in 2011. We were so new back then. They fell asleep and I put aside the Candace Bushnell novel I was reading. I carried them into their bedroom, not necessarily ours in my mind yet, and put them into bed just like I do here in Chicago seven years later. Then and now, I swell with emotion at the sound of them breathing, sleeping away the day and pain and joy, and dreaming whatever they might be dreaming. I chuckle remembering waking up the other morning. I had fallen asleep in their lap while they were reading a book Reeves recommended we check out, and I woke up the next morning with them wrapped around me. I smiled as my hand passed through their hair, my turn my love, I whispered to the shadows, the room, or maybe to them.

I rub the place between their shoulder blades. It is a small section of skin that feels like a valley. Because they are so small, their shoulder blades stick out and create a type of canyon. This structural image generates the impression that their backbone is a more like a river, powerfully swimming in its own current, pushing across the world. Within this river, nestled in a canyon of its own, I feel a sense of beauty, power, and exquisite sensuality that I've never been able to properly put into poetry or prose. I trace the edges of Linsk's spine the same way I have for years now marveling at what feels completely unique and utter perfection to the pads lucky enough to live on the tip of my fingers during these moments. I think of the way their smile lit my entire being on fire in 2011, in the moonlight asking me to marry them a few years later beside a place people go to fish or watch sunsets during family vacations, and the the sounds of Wilco's "Via Chicago" coming from their guitar the other morning when I awoke. I marvel at the ways the power of their smile, their presence, has only grown stronger and stronger in its impact on me over the years. I wonder if there is a limit it may reach at some point, but somehow, deep inside where nothing from this world can find, I know there is no such limit, not when it comes to the effervescent emotion Linsk can generate within me at any time.

REEVES

I laugh out loud both because I'm driving past a fireworks stand and because I'm moving in only a few weeks when the sounds of Wilco's "Via Chicago" come through my speakers.

I'm driving to the gallery. It is the last opening of my tenure. I'm wearing a soft pink dress shirt Ella picked out for me. I'm wearing a bracelet that speaks the rhythms of my heart. Linsk has the same bracelet. We wore them before we put rings on each other's hands in a garden in the presence of our chosen family with our co-spouse Ella smiling as she held the pillow the rings were on before she handed them to us. It was a beautiful spring day. It was the kind of garden that looks less like nature and more like an artistic rendition. It was a moment when Case just couldn't stop crying. It was a moment where Case and I competed for most happy tears, and the only such moment where I'm not sure I won the contest. Kaisa was smiling the way they do when one of the cats jumps into their lap. Michelle and Andrei wore matching outfits that day, but I never bothered to find out if there was any reason for that.

The gallery is deserted. It usually is this early in the day. The crowds and the set up and the show will come later. It's all planned out the way it should be. Linsk landed in Miami this morning. They will be here tonight too. Ella offered to come, but we both know she's knee-deep in the latest novel, so I told her not to worry about it. She sent me a novelty magnet from a place called Volumes that she says has some of the best coffee in Wicker Park. I remember Ella giving me a play-by-play one day as she dragged Case from the Stan's to Myopic Books to the Volumes place to the Reckless Records. They said they wanted me to enjoy their trip. They were nervous about something on that trip, but I don't remember what it was. We were new to each other back then, and I thought maybe she was just trying to include me.

I was still living in Orlando at the time. Linsk and I were starting to see each other. I was starting to understand the poly thing and how to interact with Ella. At one point, before the Chicago trip where they narrated the Wicker Park route via text, Ella came up to hang out with Linsk and I at a place called Stardust that sold coffee and books and maybe movies though it was always hard to tell if the movies were really for sale. I was shaking when Ella arrived. Linsk said it would be fine, but I was nervous. By the end of the night, to my surprise, Ella was cracking jokes about the three of us sharing a home in Miami and I found myself hugging her tighter than might have been good for her back. As I look at the picture of the three of us in a diner having middle of the night food and laughs during that trip, I smile at those early days. I didn't know where things were going the same way I don't know what to expect in Chicago. I just knew it felt right to let go and dive in with these people, and I guess I still feel that way. I stare at the picture, the last thing on my desk at the gallery, the only thing left to pack, and I catch the light in Linsk's eyes. There is something about that light that tells me that no matter where we go, it will be the right place as long as I can see those eyes as much as possible.

KAISA

The clouds are drifting across the sky. It reminds me of the apartment I had in Andersonville before Case and I lived together.

I would stand on the back porch staring out into the sky. I would stand there in the middle of the night when I couldn't sleep. I would stand there in the morning air listening to traffic. I would stand there when I knew Case was on the way or when my roommate was singing some country song too loud for my ears to handle. I would watch the tops and porches of the other apartments in the area. I would try to spot the place where the lady danced to New Kids on the Block every time Ella went by there for Vietnamese coffee. I would stare out into the sky and just think about the passage of years, the meaning of this or that riddle we call a part of our lives, and the thunder rumbling in the sky at seemingly random times.

Standing on the porch at the place I share with Case, I put down the Jackson Garner novel I am reading and smile. The clouds are on a journey, but it is such a slow passage that no one could guess where they are headed. I feel like that fits me. I feel like my life has been one long journey where I had no clue where I was going. I don't know how, but I feel like I landed in the right place, at least so far. I touch my chest. I do this sometimes when I'm thinking. I remember the surgery. I feel the scars that almost no one sees. I rub softly, the way I always did when this chest was, for lack of a better word, new, well, new to me at least. I think about that. It sounds like the kind of thing people say when they try a restaurant that has been in the neighborhood for fifty years. It is new, at least new to them. I watch the clouds. There is something there for me to think about, but I can't quite place what it is right now. I enjoy the quiet.

I was standing here the other night when Ella came by smelling like cigarettes, wine, and some kind of exhaust that reminded me of tractor trailer trucks. "What are you doing sunshine," I remember saying as Ella sat down on the porch beside where I'm sitting right now.

"I was hanging out with Mercury down the block, some tavern, I figured I would stop by here on the way home." Ella lit a cigarette and just sat there in the dark. I watched them. I was quiet. She was quiet. This is not unusual for us. "Case home," Ella said after fifteen minutes of silence. I said no. Case was over at Michelle's working on something for one of their projects. Ella nodded. We both looked out into the sky. I smiled at Ella. She smiled at me. We watched the sky again. The silence holding our conversations the way it usually does. This tendency to talk without talking is part of the fun we have with Jo and Case. Neither of them like quiet. Ella and I crave it sometimes. We will stare at them. We will wink and make faces at each other. We will do this outside of shops we like, such as Uncharted Books when we go there with Michelle and Jo, and just wait. You can watch them fidget and squirm in the quiet. I don't know what it feels like for them, but Ella and I silently agree that it's a lot of fun.

Tonight, it is just me out on the porch. Case is fast asleep inside. Michelle and Andrei are out on the town at some kind of wine tasting they told me about the other day. Linsk and Reeves are down in Miami at the final opening at the gallery Reeves has worked at since moving to Miami a couple years back to be with Linsk and Ella full time. Jo was here earlier playing with the cats. She's nervous because Twitter boy is coming to town for a visit later this week. Well, next week, I guess since it is the weekend and that kind of means end of the week. I don't know why that strikes me in the moment, the simple wording of it, but the clouds seem so peaceful in their quiet journey that I stop to think about it. Somewhere nearby, I think as I finally turn back toward the door and begin to move toward bed where Case awaits my presence like the missing piece of a story told in dreams, Mercury and Ella are spending the night together for the first time. I wonder if the clouds caught a glimpse of them on their passage across the sky, I like to think that's exactly what happened.

ELLA

The first night I spent with Mercury was the second time I woke up in the middle of the night at the Palmer House.

The clock on the night stand said it was just past four. Mercury was cuddled in the soft, white, flowing sheets of the bed. I was on their left. I watched them sleep. I wondered what they were dreaming. I wondered if this was a one-time thing for them while knowing it was something I hoped would only be the beginning of a never-ending adventure. There were no clothes. We left them behind earlier in the evening moving from one part of the hotel room to the other. My arm was around their waist. They warned me that sometimes they wake up in the middle of the night and have to leave, they said they don't spend the night with people. It was one of the many rules they told me about that didn't seem to apply to me so far. I woke up at least half-expecting them to already be gone. I was surprised to realize just how sad I would have been if that would have been the case. I was thrilled to see them sleeping peacefully.

The rules were an interesting source of conversation. They were more like expectations, I see now, than actual rules. They were things Mercury came up with to stay as safe as possible without feeling like they could trust anyone. I don't cry, they said. They said this, but then they fell into the deepest sobs about a night on a highway under the portico of the Cheesecake Factory on the Magnificent Mile. I don't let anyone in my house, they said. A week later they invited me into their home. I was scared because I had been hurt by someone with similar physical features in a home before, and they were scared for the same reason I later learned. I don't do well with text messages, they said. Then, they blew up my phone texting back and forth at least as fast and easily as I do since text messaging is easiest for me. I don't celebrate holidays or make plans with someone I'm dating ahead of time, they said, but we currently had plans to hang out on Record Store Day in April.

There were other rules, and I responded to each one the same. Each time, I said that was fine with me. Each time, I assumed the thing they did not do would not happen and made sure not to suggest or ask for that thing. Each time, I figured the reason didn't matter since I knew from my own experiences and those of my family that sometimes our own rules were the only things that gave us a sense of safety, structure, and consistency in the midst of a harsh world. Each time, I was surprised when the rule turned out to be unnecessary. Each time, I was surprised that they didn't need a given rule with me, or at least decided they didn't need it at a certain time once they realized I wasn't going to violate their rules in any way. I watched them sleep in the room in the Palmer House and thought about the other time I woke up in the middle of the night in this hotel to watch someone sleep and think about a somewhat new relationship.

It was back in 2012. Linsk and I had been seeing each other for less than a year. One of Linsk's co-workers and his husband had tickets to a play in Chicago at the same time we were planning to be there for work. We stayed in this hotel. Linsk had never been to Chicago. I had not yet told them I had been to Chicago. We enjoyed the play. We came back here, wrapped ourselves in blankets and each other's sense of touch, and fell into each other's eyes throughout the passage of the night. A few hours later, the clock said it was near five that night, I woke to find them cuddled against me shaking their butt in their sleep. I held them tight, like I would do now, and watched them sleep. I was scared of the feelings I had for them. I was scared I would run away from the first great thing I'd ever found, which I did a few months later to my never-ending regret. I was overcome by how strong and soft they were at the same time. I was mesmerized by the play of the lights from outside against the blankets and their skin. I watched them sleep and wondered how the hell I got so lucky. I still do that some nights when I can't fall asleep and the rhythm of their breathing punctuates the night.

Mercury wiggles in their sleep. They push their head into my shoulder. They sigh, a sound I've learned is a positive one in their vocal delivery. I feel the warmth of their body and slide back in time a few hours. I came into the room after them. I had been downstairs having a cigarette and debating whether or not to get a coffee. I was nervous about being alone with them in this room. I was nervous about being with them in a new way for the first time. There was a part of the me that visited this city the first time that always assumed sex, or maybe some other temporary good, was all people ever really wanted from me. It was the end of March, and the previous month or so with Mercury was far more fun and emotional than I would have expected ahead of time. I realized I was nervous because being close to them felt important to me. I put out my cigarette, but it took me longer to make my way upstairs than it should have.

Mercury laughs under their breath in between stretches of their shoulder, the right one. I wonder for a moment if they're waking up, but their breathing returns to the sleepy rhythm within moments. I entered the hotel room unsure what I would find. It was the same kind, maybe even the same one, I couldn't remember, that Linsk and I stayed in years before this night. It was the kind of suite where it begins with an opening room and then continues into the bedroom, more like an apartment than a classic hotel room, I guess. I walked into the suite and found Mercury perched on top of the desk in the front part of the room. I stopped. I stared. I was amazed in all the right ways. We had been joking the week before about an image they had of me writing at a desk, composing the next great story, and how much fun it would be for them to sit on my desk and feel my fingers caressing them instead of the keyboard.

I feel the soft, shuddering movement of Mercury's ribs beneath their back muscles as they lean deeper into my body while continuing to sleep and maybe dream. I stared at them on the top of the desk for what seemed like a lifetime. I didn't think about it, I just moved toward them, into them, and as our bodies connected, I felt a twin series of moans and sighs escape us both as if they'd been begging for release. Mercury dug into my back as I stood between their muscular, sensual thighs grasping the powerful muscles that made up their lower back. We parted for a moment and they said to wait. I waited. They disappeared into the bathroom in between the two rooms that made up the suite. They came back without clothing, as naked as when we violated another of their rules by holding each other in their bed the week before when they felt the desire to be close to me even though we weren't ready for more conventional sexual activity yet. They smiled at me. I smiled back. They grabbed my hands, and pulled me, forcefully and softly at the same time.

As Mercury says my name in their sleep, I remember the way the structure of the bed seemed to morph into the perfect hammock holding our connected bodies as we hit the sheets. My clothes disappeared in a series of sounds, tastes, and sensations. I couldn't breathe and yet my breathing was harder and louder than usual. The curve of their hip met the angular dip in my shoulders as I felt their back arch and reached into a garden of sensations captured in the expanse of their perfectly relaxed and vibrating skin. The sheets went haywire. Protective necessities we agreed upon in the weeks prior found use in the mixture of touches, tickles, and tastes that blocked out the sounds and sights of the city somewhere, seemingly far away, outside of our room, our embrace, our dance together through rhythmic pulses of one another. The gasps, from them, from me, from us, shattered the other potential sounds of the night. Together, we grabbed, held, and called for each other, for the sunshine hiding in the night, or maybe just for the sweet explosion contained within the connection of our desires.

MERCURY

The sun felt different when I woke up in the Palmer House.

I was watching the sky from the window of the room I shared with Ella. I was surprised I was still in the room. My own experiences with sexual activity had not been what I would have called romantic in any way, and I rarely spent the night with anyone. Ella was wrapped in the blankets on the much-softer-than-what-I-can-afford-for-my-graduate-school-apartment-bed in the middle of this part of the suite. I was surprised to be in such a nice place. I was surprised that I didn't want to leave. I wanted to watch Ella wake up, to feel her coming to consciousness again. I was nervous when she told me she booked the room. I didn't want the first time to happen at my shitty apartment or the home she shares with Linsk and will share with Reeves. I needed a neutral site. I was surprised she said the Palmer House, but she seemed to know it well. On the one hand, this meant it was okay that I had never been in this hotel. On the other hand, I wondered if that meant this kind of thing was normal for her and I was just the latest hook-up to be tossed aside once she got bored with me. I was sure she was going to get bored with me.

Ella kicks her right leg out from under the covers. I'm trying to remember, as I will tell her later, the last time I slept so well. I can feel and smell and taste her on me as I stand by the window, I want to keep these senses forever. That thought, while true, scares me. This was not how I expected things to go when she confessed her undying love to me weeks ago. There are so many things I have gotten in the habit of not doing, my rules as I call them, but none of them make any sense with Ella. She doesn't even seem to mind them, and somehow, that makes them seem even more useless. I think about letting her into my home for the first time. I don't do that. I don't like people to know exactly where I live, but I guess Ella isn't people to me. Maybe, instead, after long searching, maybe she's more like *my people.*

I crawl into the bed, the soft sheets cuddling my knees, and start rubbing Ella's back. She almost purrs for lack of a better description of the sound she makes. I save the sound, lock it in my collection of memories, something to play on repeat on a rainy day. I don't know, but I like having her in my shitty apartment that she somehow never makes fun of or seems to think is all that shitty. I think about her holding me the other night. The nightmares had been bad. It was worse than when I broke down crying like an idiot at the Cheesecake Factory. Ella held me at the Cheesecake Factory and the other night in my bed. There was something magical about being naked and not being afraid that I wish I could put into words. I don't know if I've felt that ever, or maybe just not since I was too little to remember. She held me, naked in her arms, and I just somehow knew that I was safe, and I could relax.

I wish I could have had some of that relaxation as I arrived here last night. Ella wiggles her butt the way I've seen her do to make Linsk giggle. It's the tiniest little motion because she basically has no butt, but something about it is endearing. She's breathing softly. Sleep is her friend this morning. It was mine earlier, but before that, we arrived at the hotel and I was glad she wanted to have a smoke so I could check out the room myself. I thought about running away, but instead, I kept remembering a fantasy I told her about. In the fantasy, she is writing at a desk, working on some story, maybe one about me in my most hopeful moments, and I sit on the desk without any clothes on. I ask her if she wants a break. She smiles at me. I pull her into me, and we take a break from the world within each other. I've been having this dream, as I accidentally told her while I got drunk at some tavern, since we first met. I thought she would laugh at me, but she said it sounded beautiful. I think about that moment, her smile as I drunkenly recounted my fantasy, and I change into a robe and perch myself on top of the desk in the front room, or maybe living room, of the suite. I wait.

Remembering that she said it was okay when we talked about consent, boundaries, protection, and other details related to sexual activity, I begin softly kissing her breasts while she sleeps. I feel her body respond. Her hand rubs the top of my head. I was so scared sitting on the desk. When Ella walked in, she just stared at me and I didn't know what to say or do. I thought that maybe I had made a mistake. I thought she was going to laugh at me. I thought I was being stupid. I wanted to disappear as fast as possible and run away never looking back. It felt like she stared at me, sitting on the desk feeling like an idiot, for years, but I know it was only a few moments. I was about to apologize or say something when she moved across the room faster than I thought she could move. She wrapped me in her arms, our pelvic muscles bouncing against each other like well-trained dancers in the middle of a hot club scene, and our lips connected in an explosion brighter than the sunlight this morning.

I run my hand down Ella's stomach while continuing to nibble on her as if I'm eating an extra-tasty cookie that must be savored for all its glory. I feel her squirm and giggle and moan softly. Her eyes open as she softly says my name, continues rubbing my head with her hand, and moves her other hand to my chest in a sweet, sensual motion that makes my heart tingle beneath my ribs. I don't know how long we were making out on the desk. I felt like my whole body was alive and on fire at the same time. I needed a moment, so I told her to wait, and Ella smiled at me as she pulled back without question. Something about that gave me courage and I went into the bathroom, stared at myself for a moment thinking this was really happening, and dropped the robe and my underwear on the floor. I came out from the bathroom making a beckoning motion to Ella. She again came to me faster than I would have expected and together we half-wrestled, half-danced, half-floated to the bedroom.

I feel Ella's lips finding my shoulder. I feel her body shiver in response to my touch. I feel her quiver. She says good morning. I smile at her. I straddle her and feel our bodies hugging each other in a magical embrace that blocks out everything else. I felt adrenaline and calm surge somehow at the same time as our bodies connected only a few hours ago. I felt my inner self, whatever that is, shiver and grab at the same time, I just wanted more, more Ella, more connection, more raw feelings, more of life! It was like I had been reborn as if part of me had been hidden and buried for too long, like the sun that morning, I felt different and while it was scary, it was a difference I wanted to grab hold of and ride through the world.

CASE

I feel like doing ethnographic research for a living has changed me in ways I did not expect or even notice right away.

It's like I see things that I didn't see before. I guess that's what learning new skills is supposed to be like. I was telling Ella about it one night, and she said observation is too difficult for most people to pay much attention to. I'm on my way to look at books because I have a couple fresh bills in my pocket. I'm in the mood for the kind of thriller Alice Sebold would be proud to write or maybe a Pearl Cleage book that will blow my mind in unexpected ways. Jo says she wants a life that would find voice in a novel by some esoteric writer with no hope left and just enough optimism to see this as a good thing. Ella says she wants only the types of love affairs that would fit neatly into a Damien Rice song. Linsk says they only want memories that are worth turning into poetry. Michelle says she wants to understand why she is always trying to understand things. I just want to read books and watch people.

Just for fun, I get off at a train stop I'm not familiar with and begin roaming around. I see the usual shops and in-a-hurry people you see at every stop, but for some reason I take a left and find myself walking through a park. I turn on my observational eyes. What is here, what is happening, a city alive on a Saturday afternoon – what is there to take from this. I see flowers in the trees, a picnic area that serves as what appears to be a Latin barbershop, and highways that provide background noise for the neighborhood. I watch older men of varied races play and curse about a "friendly" game of chess, and I stop to stare at a wall by the basketball courts that is decorated with a mural about past glory. I see a shuffleboard court, common in Florida, less common here, covered in puddles and providing a mirror image of tennis courts nearby. I see bright shades of color where someone has painted "imagine" on the concrete. I see a school across the street, and an elder man with an Italian accent curses at everything and nothing at the same time. A younger person carrying the same accent apologizes to everyone within hearing of the elder man's diatribe. There is a pool that only a few people are using and a makeshift bicycle repair shop where a young black kid is detailing any bike that comes to him. I don't want to stop, but I wonder what the kid thinks of all the activity around him. An old man plays the trumpet from his wheelchair. He is better than okay, but not all that great at the same time. He has a Koran in his lap. He sits facing ball fields across the street. The fields look lonely, but they recall their better days with signs and markers celebrating former players and games. I smile as I reach the end of the park, this is why I wanted to live in a city in the first place.

MICHELLE

"What are you doing," I say into the phone as I reach the Logan Square station.

"I'm just roaming around the city thinking, but I may go to a bookstore soon because I want to get a new novel," Case says with a whimsical joy embedded in their voice. "What are you up to?"

"I just finished having a great lunch with Linsk, we're going to do some health outreach in poor neighborhoods in the coming month, I think I want ice cream," I say smiling and beginning to walk down the stairs, "But none of that frozen yogurt bullshit."

"How about Jeni's, that way I can go to Myopic and use some of my store credit," Case says in that way they always talk when they're nervous, really fast, all the words jumbled together as if they are certain the listener will hit them in the face with a newspaper or at least that's how it sounds to me when they're anxious, "Or, well, I mean, we can go anywhere I guess, but I was thinking if you're over near your house I can meet you in Wicker."

"That sounds great," I say using my most positive voice. I know what it's like to be anxious at times, though not like Case, and I want to reassure them. "I'm at the Logan station, I'll meet you at the Stan's right by the Wicker stop we usually go to with Ella."

"Sounds good to me," Case says, and we get off the phone. For a moment, I think about texting them to see how long they will be, but I don't worry about it. I get on the train to find some fucking asshat staring at my ass, fuck you, I want to scream but I just ignore him, just another day in the city, I got used to this shit when I lived in New York while getting my master's degree before coming here to fight like a damn dog to get and protect decent healthcare access for women who shouldn't have to fight for it in the first damn place. I pull out my methodological notebook that I don't call a journal because journal sounds too emotional. I start taking notes on ways to advertise programs with the resources Linsk has access to through the center they are working at now that they live in the city. I get off the train at the Damen stop.

I go inside the Stan's and there is Ella eating one of those disgusting Captain Crunch donuts and talking to Jo about something that I can't make out at first. Ella waves me over. I hold up a hand, order a coffee and a sensible glazed donut, and go to the counter on the edge of the shop to fix my coffee. "What's up," I say as I slide into the chair on the other side of Ella from where Jo is sitting.

"Jo is taking over my life, but maybe in a good way," Ella says laughing before taking a sip of her coffee and smiling at the feeling of Jo punching her in the shoulder in response to the smartass remark. "We're just trading notes, what about you?"

"I'm meeting Case over here to get some ice cream and go by Myopic."

"Ooh, there is a great frozen yogurt place over by Myopic that," Jo starts to say before Ella lets out a series of roaring laughs and I try to keep from choking the both of them. "What," Jo says, "What's so damn funny?"

"Michelle has a deep, well earned, hatred for frozen yogurt."

"I don't do that bullshit," I say laughing in spite of myself. My mother took me for frozen yogurt every week when I was a kid. My mom was my hero. I worshiped her and loved her more than I thought it was possible to love anyone before finding Andrei, Case, and the rest of our ragtag bunch of misfits and lovers. She's the reason I went into healthcare. She's the reason I try to save every damn woman I can who gets stuck in our healthcare system. She has been dead for twenty years, but I still hear her voice inside my head every day. I know she would be proud of me. I know that she loved me with all she had. I know that she loved frozen yogurt, but there are some things that I only shared with her and I like to keep those things for just the two of us. Ella knows all this – she didn't eat ice cream for years due to her own traumatic experience with it as a child. She smiles at me. I smile back. I miss my mom every day.

"There is a story here," Jo says smiling, "I know there is."

I'm about to tell her the story, but at that moment, Case arrives, and I think, next time. I'm still kind of surprised how easy it has gotten to talk about these things. There was a time when anything to do with my mom was off limits, I just didn't talk about her at all. I thought that was good, at first, like I was preserving her for me, for all time. Over time, though, I realized that I missed talking about her and not talking about her felt like it made me miss her even more. I finally started telling Andrei about her the first year we were dating, and something about that experience, and the way he seemed to both understand and care about everything I would share about her, led me to slowly, little-by-little, share her with others in my life in the years since that time. I smile thinking about how happy she would be with my work and if she could see me surrounded by these people who love me. It aches, missing her, and it always will, I guess, but the ache is something, like everything else about her, that I just want to have and hang onto so she always stays close to me in any way she can. I smile at the others as Case makes their way through the door to the shop. They come toward us while sliding, almost slipping and falling, across the donut shop with a smile and a look in their eyes that tells me a joke is coming as well. "So, are we having donuts or going to get some not-that-frozen-yogurt-bullshit," they say to the delight, and laughter, of Ella and Jo. If I'm being completely honest with you, then, okay, I admit it, I chuckled a little bit too.

JO

Twitter boy came for a visit the second weekend of April. It was fun. I have more to say about it, but I'm still trying to avoid thinking about how much I like him, so we'll get to that. I mean, it's only been two weeks since the visit, I have time to think about it later.

Case is sitting on the other side of the table at the New Wave coffeeshop. They are working on the transcripts from one of their dissertation interviews. They are studying the ways asexual or ace people make sense of identity. They are doing that thing where they chew on their pen. They have three color pencils to the side of their notebook, their dissertation notebook they call it, which seems like just another journal, but I guess it's not, but maybe it is. That's the way some things are, right? They look like anything else, but they are special. That's what it's like with Twitter boy. He seems like any other boy, but he's not. Other boys have been such assholes, but he's like sweet and funny and I'm not sure what the hell to do with sweet and funny, asshole I know how to handle, I have practice with that, years of practice. I don't want to think about this right now.

I flip a page in my Billie Letts novel, it's the one about the orphans. I watch Linsk sipping their tea talking to Michelle about some new initiative. They both work in health. Michelle does mostly reproductive health stuff of some sort that goes over my head. Linsk goes even more over my head, sometimes it feels like I love them without even having met them yet, that's how far over all our heads their thinking goes. The two of them are huddled over flyers they designed for outreach for southside medical clinics. I watch the ends of Linsk's blonde hair fall against the edge of their forehead. I watch Michelle's slender frame, captured in a jeans and striped-shirt combo, adjust in her seat. They look like they're in rhythm, like they're making music with their collaborative work or something like that, a poet could say it better. That's the thing about the Twitter boy stuff, I know I could make more sense of it if I was just more creative. I need that kind of poetic juice that the romantic types have. Did I ever have that? Was it in me, but ripped away by the assholes? I don't know, I don't want to think about it.

Andrei is fiddling with some machine, one of the ones he uses to make this or that beat at this or that moment. I can see him just barely outside. He's on the last of the wooden benches near the tables that come out when the weather and the city regulations allow them to. He's sitting beside Ella. She's gesturing with her right hand the way she does when she tries to make a point. Andrei is laughing at her or with her, I can't tell from here. There is an ease in his movements, hands grabbing the block lines that make up the machine, that seems sweet to me, I don't know why. These things I don't know bother me, I'm like Case that way. For example, I don't know what Twitter boy thought of our visit. I don't know if we'll be together again soon or later or something in between. I don't know why everything reminds me of him right now when I really don't want to think about any of that stuff.

I try to distract myself further by looking to the left. I think about getting one of the pressed sandwiches Ella gets here all the time. I think of this because I can now see Reeves and Kaisa sitting in the front window on the other side of the shop, the side without the benches. I never know which is front and which is back in this store. Reeves is eating one of those pressed sandwiches. He's in town for the weekend and to bring some more of his stuff. I watch Kaisa adjust their glasses, their bulky, athletic frame seeming tiny in comparison to the size of Reeves. The contrast reminds me of the way I feel with Twitter boy and without him. When he's around I feel more peaceful if that makes any damn sense, but without him, like now, I can't stop thinking about anything and everything that crosses my mind. What is that? Ella would know. I should ask her. I don't want to ask her. I'm too tired to think about this.

Luckily, I have a distraction! Looking way too scared for words, at least to my eyes but maybe I'm channeling the first time I was around the whole family, Mercury comes walking through the door on the side without the benches. I smile at them. They give me their fake, I'm-not-sure-what-the-hell-I'm-doing-here smile, and I wave them over. I told them we would all be here this afternoon, but I didn't think they'd come by. They take two steps toward me, but then they stop and I'm pretty sure they're going to make a run for it. I start to get up, but Linsk has already spotted them. I'm always amazed by how fast Linsk can move. They cross the coffeeshop and suddenly appear right in front of Mercury smiling at them, giving them a hug, and walking them to the bar to get a coffee. I can tell Mercury is shaking the same way I was shaking when Twitter boy hugged me at the airport. Damnit! I don't want to think about that.

LINSK

"I think these materials will work perfectly, I mean, they get to the point and the people in the community will have no trouble using them," Michelle says looking over the flyers we created together for a health outreach program we're doing for the southside clinics.

We're sitting in the New Wave coffeehouse in Logan Square on April 28th. The place is only a few blocks from her house and mine, so we decided to make it our working spot. Ella is in love with Same Day Café around the corner and after meeting Case and Andrei for lunch there, her and Reeves came by too at about the same time Jo and Kaisa arrived after having lunch at the Chicago Diner. It is fun seeing everybody here, spread out into their own little worlds, at the same time. I watch the room in between sips of my tea and words Michelle and I trade like the latest round of a debate because we both talk too fast for most people in sentences that Ella says feel more like essays written by some speech writer in our heads before we speak. I'm watching Jo because she seems like she has something on her mind when I follow her eyes to the front door. There is Mercury, fresh from spending the weekend with Ella celebrating Record Store Day a week ago today and looking terrified.

"Hold that thought," I say to Michelle hopping up from the table. I remember the way Reeves talked about meeting all of us together for the first time. I remember how overwhelming it felt to him. There were so many of us and we were so close to each other. He said it was like the first time he felt like he had a family, but it was also terrifying because he was so worried he wouldn't be accepted, or he would say something wrong, especially around Ella. These thoughts flash through my head as I cross the coffeeshop moving at my normal, casual pace because rushing might further spook Mercury. Behind them to the right, I see Reeves and Kaisa sitting together talking and they both catch my eye and see where I'm going. They each start to get up, and out of the corner of my eye I can see Jo motioning for Mercury to come on over to her. I think of Ella sleeping this morning with the little stuffed duck Mercury got her curled up in her arms, and I smile as I arrive right in front of Mercury just as they seem to start to turn.

The turn stops abruptly as I say, "Well, glad you could make it out here little crow," and wrap them in a hug that allows me to feel the stress draining out of their body. They smiled the first time I called them a little crow when they were picking up Ella at the house last week. I told them that when I think of Mercury, I think of a Counting Crows song by the same name. They were unfamiliar with the band or the song, but I think they liked having a nickname from me. I know Reeves loved it when Ella referred to him as juicy muscles, a bonding kind of thing. "Why don't we get you a coffee you can drink faster than the speed of light?"

I watch them giggle, blush, and relax even more. We head over to the bar to get them a small coffee. It has already become a running joke in the family that Mercury drinks their coffee like a trucker trying to shave minutes off his break at a truck stop. "By the time you finish ordering your own drink," Case said laughing, "They are done with theirs and just kind of looking around to see what they're supposed to do next." Jo falls in step with us as we reach the bar. We get Mercury a coffee with some half and half and two Splendas. We also get them a cheese Danish because Ella said they like those and Jo swears by the ones at this place.

As we turn around from the bar, Reeves is standing in front of us. I give him a soft kiss and watch Mercury blush the way they do when Ella kisses them in front of me. I remember Reeves getting used to the poly thing too and smile. I watch Jo put her arm around Mercury and then Reeves introduces himself. As if slipping on their words in a moment of awkwardness made for a romantic comedy, Mercury says, "So, your juicy muscles," and we all start laughing while their face takes on a shade of red most often seen on the neon signs of the Las Vegas strip. Reeves giggles and pulls Mercury in for a hug. The blush begins to dissipate, but the laughter continues when Jo says, "Just wait until juicy muscles bursts into tears because you say something nice at the right moment, and you'll get to see him match you blush for blush."

REEVES

Even a few hundred feet away, the smooth slope of Linsk's long, skinny legs peeking out from under the slip that they wear as a dress because dresses often aren't made small enough for them leaves me having trouble keeping up with what Kaisa is saying.

Kaisa is talking about having me do an art installation with some kids they work with in the southern part of the city. I watch Linsk cross their legs and remember the feeling of those legs around my waist this morning. I smile at Kaisa. I finish the sandwich Ella recommended. It was better than I expected. Kaisa is explaining their idea for the project with the community. I love this idea, but I'm so distracted. Linsk always distracts me. Linsk is working on health care plans with Michelle and something about the way they shine when their mind is firing at all cylinders just moves me out of the moment and into a type of trance. I smile at Kaisa and ask what the installation would involve. It took more effort than it should have to figure out how to ask that question. Kaisa explains the idea for a mural. I like murals, but I've only done one so far. I explain that I think we can do it and that it will be great, but that I'll need to brush up on my skills. Kaisa says the plan would be for the summer. We agree that could work out well and it would give me time to prepare and get the right materials.

I watch as Linsk suddenly pops out of their chair the way they do when they've just remembered something important. At first, I think they're coming over to where Kaisa and I are sitting against the window in the front of the coffeeshop. They're moving faster than most people, but that is not all that fast for them. They are focused on something, but I realize quickly that it is not us or the window we're sitting in. I see Kaisa's eyes move to where it looks like Linsk is looking and I recognize the buzz cut and Billy Moon t-shirt I have heard Ella talk about. Mercury took Jo and Ella's invitation to come out today and see us all. Wow, I think, that takes courage. I start to get up and smile as I see Kaisa doing the same thing. My mind goes back to the sight of Case sitting on the porch in Miami looking at me like I was some kind of predator in the jungle as I arrived at a party at Ella and Linsk's house, later our house.

I remember that night so long ago that seems like yesterday as I move across the coffeeshop to catch up with Linsk and Mercury at the bar. Case looked at me in a way that made me equally terrified and grateful for them at the same time. I wanted to choke the shit out of them for being so scary and suspicious, and at the same time, I wanted to wrap them in an everlasting hug for being so protective of these wonderful people I was falling in love with. I make it up to the bar, as if I'm Kaisa answering the door that night in Miami, to be the first to say hello. Linsk gives me a beautiful kiss that spins my head around and curls my toes, and I can't help but tear up a bit as I watch Mercury blush the same way I did at first when Ella and Linsk would kiss in front of me. It seems so natural now, but it was such a new thing for me at the time. There was this one time I was trying to get into the door of the house in Miami and I almost fell over trying to give them space as they were kissing. It was so awkward for me then, but somehow the difficulty dissipated. I guess it's the same for Mercury today.

"Hey Mercury, or maybe I should say little crow," I say smiling. Linsk smiles at me, and I add, "I remember how awkward right now can be, but welcome to the family and trust me it gets easier." I watch them kind of drop whatever mask they were wearing. It's like I can see the soft, sweet, caring person Ella is in love with for just a moment, and then, as fast as it wavered a second before, the mask is back, trying to appear cool and calm. I remember that dance, mask on then off then on, as well. I smile at them. They blush and smile back.

"So, your juicy muscles," they ask, and I know they'll fit into this family perfectly. They have the same deflection and smart ass sense of humor that bond the rest of us together. I recognize the tactic. Ella and Linsk are experts at it. There are still times where either of them will feel emotional or shy or embarrassed and quickly turn to some very sarcastic or otherwise hilarious statements to shift the discussion elsewhere. I just cry. That's what I do. I'm the one who just loses it emotionally, well, now that I don't try to drown the emotions via way too much alcohol anymore the way Ella once snorted hers with too much cocaine. I just giggle in response to them and give them a light hug, well, light for me. They smile at me. I smile at them. I think on some level we both know that we each understand this moment in a way that many other people might not be able to make sense of without the experience.

As we let go of each other, I watch as Kaisa moves through the laughter around us to give Mercury a hug. Mercury beams in Kaisa's arms while Linsk pats them on the back. Jo makes some comment that I don't catch, but it has something to do with me being emotional and I blush, and everyone laughs and inside I laugh and feel warm. Linsk smiles at me in a way that only they seem to be able to – a way that sets the blood in my veins on fire and makes it feel like anything or maybe just everything is possible even if only for a few moments. I smile back at them and watch Kaisa lead Mercury to where Michelle has pushed a couple tables together, so we can all sit in one place for a little while and get to know each other.

KAISA

"I remember how awkward right now can be, but welcome to the family and trust me it gets easier," Reeves says to Mercury as we stand by the bar in New Wave.

I remember this all too well. I remember that Ella and Linsk flew me down to Florida to spend a week with them and Case. I remember feeling like there was no way I would get through that week without ruining everything. I was as desperately in love with Case as I am now, but not even as good at showing it as I am now. Showing emotions was dangerous in my life before Case, I had to learn how to do it with them. I went to Florida. I was terrified. I knew that everything I thought was wrong with me would come out by the end of the trip. I just knew this, but of course, sometimes what we know is only what we fear. I was wrong. It was one of the most wonderful times of my life. I remember crying, what few tears my body will let me generate, on the plane back to Chicago. I remember I felt like I found a place I finally did belong and exist fully, but I also remembered how terrifying it was.

I give Mercury a hug. They bury their face in my shoulder the way they did after spending the night over at mine and Case's place watching bad movies with Ella and us after spending the day roaming through record stores last Saturday. Jo makes a joke about how emotional Reeves is before going back to the counter to pick up a Danish of some sort. Linsk is grinning at all of us, that same grin I remember from the first time Case and I kissed in front of them. Reeves is blushing. I wonder if he'll cry. Mercury's athletic body shakes in my arms, just a little, I know that shake and I hold them closer. I whisper, "You're doing great, and we're all happy you're here," in their ear and feel them shake even more. I know that shake too. They don't believe this is real yet, but they will, it will sink in and nothing will ever be the same again, they won't ever have to feel alone again.

I remember when Reeves first showed up. I say showed up like it was some predestined turn of events, but that's how it felt. I guess maybe that's how I felt to Case, Ella, and Linsk. I opened the door that day he visited the four of us in Miami. Case was sitting outside like a pit bull watching for his arrival. They were doing their best impersonation of Linsk, the roaring lion that protects all of us all the time the same way Ella takes care of us and Reeves cries for us. I guess we all play our roles in this family. I opened the door. I saw the fear in his eyes. I remember just wanting to make things easier for him in any way I could. I think about that as I watch Case and Michelle move chairs and tables together out of the corner of my eye. Jo puts the Danish down on one of the tables beside where Case is sitting. I remember going with Case to get books and noodles with Jo the first time. I remember the same loneliness in Jo's eyes that no longer gets to live there, no longer squatting inside her rent free, no longer allowed when she knows she can reach for any or all of us at any moment if she wants to. I can too.

I lead Mercury over to the set of tables. We sit down together. I put my hand in the outstretched hand Case offers in the seat beside the one I chose. Michelle beams and practically screams hello to Mercury while handing them the Danish that Jo had left on the other table. Reeves and Linsk sit down on the other side of Mercury creating a lack of empty space on the side of Michelle opposite where Case is sitting. That seems fitting, I think, that image. There was emptiness, spaces with nothing to show for them, but then we found each other, or maybe Ella found us all or Linsk did, I don't know, but we found each other, and little-by-little the space, the emptiness and loneliness, evaporated like the last drops of rain at the tail end of a hurricane that you were sure would destroy everything in its path.

MERCURY

I must have stood on the corner of Logan and Milwaukee for an hour.

That's not true, but it felt like forever. I got a text from Ella. She said she was going over to a place called New Wave with the rest of the family. I got a text from Jo. She said she was going to be at a place called New Wave with the family. They both invited me to come along and hang out with everyone. This was not something I thought I should do. Linsk was intimidating enough to win a war by themselves, and I was still far more emotional than I was comfortable with around Kaisa and Case. I didn't know how I would react around Reeves, and I wasn't sure what to make of Michelle or Andrei. I could still smell Ella in my sheets from the night before. After she left, the nightmares were not as bad but still terrible. I was tired. I wished I had a good reason not to go, but I was pretty sure that only fear would come up if I tried to form one.

I could have gotten to Logan Square a few different ways. I knew this by now. I had spent nights with Ella in the neighborhood at the house she shared with Linsk and would share with Reeves. This had been mostly when Linsk was out of town. I had met Linsk, before and after Ella and I started, what do you call it, dating I guess, but it was still scary. I admired them so much, I wonder if that made it even harder. I thought about going to a bar near my apartment and drinking so much that I wouldn't recognize myself or my name for days if I managed to survive long enough to try to remember what the hell happened. I thought about drowning in the sweet cough-medicine-type-taste of liquor clouding my Diet Coke. Instead, I got on the red line telling myself that I would just see what happened. I figured I would get off in the loop, change my mind, and go back home with a bottle or forty-six of them and go to bed. That's what credit cards are for, I said to myself laughing as I got off the train in the loop.

I surprised myself by getting on the blue line in the loop. I didn't think I would. I thought about stopping in Wicker Park and going to the Pasta Bowl. Ella and I ate there one night. She kissed me on the sidewalk outside of the place. I could go there. Sit outside and remember the kiss. I could then go to Reckless in Wicker. We stopped there making our way through the city looking at records on Record Store Day last weekend. Maybe I would keep the tour of nostalgic Ella places going and hit the Exchange and Shuga Records too. I thought about this until a few minutes after the doors closed and we left the Damen stop continuing toward Logan Square. I thought about just going forward past Logan. Ella had mentioned a large mall off of one of the blue line stops, but I couldn't remember which stop. I'd always found airports comforting in their anonymity, maybe I could just keep going to the end of the line.

When I got off the train at the Logan Square Station, I kind of expected some kind of storm or natural disaster to take place. I'm not sure why I felt this way, but I did. I thought about going in the opposite direction of New Wave. My phone said it was to the right. I could go to the left instead. I went to the right. I walked much slower than I normally did. In fact, I giggled and maybe even blushed when I realized I was walking even slower than Ella does after all the times I made fun of how slow Ella moved through the city. I remembered being on this road with Ella when we went to Uncharted Books because Ella likes to look at her books sitting on shelves waiting for new friends to pick them up for a date. That's how Ella says it. It makes me giggle just thinking about it. I stand in the middle of the intersection for a moment, and then cross the street. The New Wave place is just ahead of me. I stand still for much longer than I have any reason to on that corner. I think about going over to the other book store Ella showed me, the one by Lula Café, what was it, oh yeah, City Lit. I think about doing that, but instead I start walking straight toward the entrance of the New Wave place.

When I walk in the door, I see Jo right away and I also spot Linsk and Michelle. I don't see Ella, but already, it seems like too many people. I feel too much. I'm not used to feeling anything. I'm used to drinking away the feelings. Somewhere in the back of my head, I hear her speak to me from that old creepy highway all those years ago, I don't want to think about her right now. That's the problem with feelings, whenever I feel them, she is not far behind. I shake my head.

I shouldn't have come here. This is a mistake. I start to turn around and leave. Jo has seen me, but she'll understand, she won't hate me too much. I tell myself this until I feel a presence as if by magic, and there is Linsk standing right in front of me. I just stare at them as they say something, what did they say, I try to hear them, I cannot. I just stare.

There is a flurry of motion that is mostly a blur in my mind. I feel so much. I tear up at least fifty-six times, but I can't tell if anyone notices. If you start crying and your face turns red, but no one sees it, did it really happen? I don't know. I find myself at the bar. I don't order. Linsk does that for me. That's good. I'm not sure I can talk. I find myself being hugged by Reeves who doesn't seem to hate me at all like I thought he should. I remember him and Linsk kissing so softly, kind of like Linsk and Ella or Ella and me, but not the same either, their own kind of kiss. Jo is with me and then she's not and then she has a Danish for some reason. Michelle is smiling at me. She moves tables with the help of Case and I feel Kaisa. Kaisa holds me the way Kaisa does, like how Ella does but not the same, the same feeling of comfort, like I get from Linsk too, but also not the same, our kind of hug maybe, I don't know. Everything is blurry, it's hard to breathe, I'm sitting at a table. There was an empty space, but then there is no empty space and they're all there and none of them seem to hate me and I don't know what to do with that, so I just sit there, and we talk but I'm not sure what anyone says.

MICHELLE

"I just thought it made sense to build our own table," I say to Case as we sit down.

Mercury looks both so cute and so overwhelmed. I text Andrei to tell him that they came after all, we had a bet on it and that bastard guessed right. That's okay, I'll go to his stupid little film screening thing that he keeps talking about nonstop. I was going to go with him anyway. I love the guy; I just like giving him hell. Case sits beside me on one side and Jo is on the other side. Jo has a Danish that she slides to Mercury. Mercury eats it so fast it reminds me of the summer's I spent with my dad at truck stops where the guys came in, ate, and left in the span of maybe five minutes sometimes. I wonder when Andrei will come inside. He won't be long. I feel an ache when I think of my recent trip to Texas. I don't say it much, but it's hard to be away from Andrei for a while, we center each other in some way, or at least that's what Ella says.

A Royal Thunder song starts playing in the New Wave. I wonder about the pressed sandwiches they sell, but I'm not hungry enough for a whole sandwich. Am I hungry? It's hard to tell. I try to think of something to add to the conversation, but it seems to be moving too fast for me to keep up with or maybe I'm just nervous or hungry. I wish I could think of something to say, but I just watch Reeves rubbing Linsk's back as he says something about a mural and Kaisa nods and Case hops up and leaves then comes back with a cup of water. "So, how do you like living in Uptown," I say in the general direction of Mercury.

They smile and blush and say, "I just found out it was called that the other day."

"You live in the same building Case used to live in," Linsk says smiling and nuzzling Reeves in the process, "Ella said you're on a different floor, Case, is that the one with the rats?"

"No," Case says laughing as they lean forward in their seat, "That was in Pilsen."

"Where's Pilsen," Reeves asks taking a sip of his tea.

"It's on the pink line," Andrei says coming up behind me, "We'll take you out there one day, some cool spots in between the rats." Andrei puts his arms around me and kisses me on the cheek. I watch Ella come around the table and give Mercury a soft kiss on the lips. If I didn't know better, I would swear Mercury melted a little and blushed and then looked at Linsk as fast as humanly possible like Reeves when he was getting used to the poly thing from what I've heard from Case and Kaisa. Linsk smiles and Ella blows them a kiss. Mercury puts their hand in Ella's hand and Kaisa says something about missing Case's old apartment. Case was living there when the two of them were getting to know each other. It has special meaning. I feel that way about mine and Andrei's apartment in Logan, but we may move at some point.

ANDREI

The sun is sweeping across the tops of the building as Ella and I sit outside New Wave.

The rest of the family is inside. It's one of those few days where all of us come to the same place. I wonder if these days will be more frequent now that we're all in the same city. Michelle and Linsk are inside working, as usual, and the others are each doing their own thing. I've been outside with Ella debating the merits of this or that audio equipment for about an hour. Ella read a couple books on the subject and wanted my take on things. It never ceases to amaze me that she is literally the most curious person I've ever met. Ella tosses a cigarette while staring up at the corner. She has a smile on her face. The sun captures the image perfectly. I rub the rag I brought with me over the new board I picked up, well new to me though used by others, at the swap meet they were having over off the California stop the other day. It was the oddest thing. I just stumbled across the series of tables with merchandise on them and could not help but look. I guess that is the point of a pop-up type market, but this is the first time I've found anything worth remembering or buying at one of those things, so it feels special.

I watch a group of teenagers come down the road on skateboards. I wonder how much fun they are having and think about trying out some skateboarding myself. Ella is putting her stuff in her bag. She lights another smoke, turns back to the corner, and smiles again. I wonder what she sees, if anything. I've learned over time that sometimes she just stares off into space for no particular reason. Other times, it's almost like she sees things that other people miss. She blows out smoke and taps her foot against the wooden rail that encircles the seating area. I'm about to say something when my phone goes off in my pocket. I check it. That's what Ella was looking at, I think, and then I say, "Michelle says Mercury is here."

"I know," Ella says smiling and taking another drag off the smoke. "You want to go inside and say hello." She throws out the cigarette, fastens the clips on her bag, and smiles at me. I nod, and we leave the porch. I never know if this is the front or the back of New Wave, but I also never bother to ask. Maybe it's better not to know some things, I think, as we move indoors and head for the two tables set up in the front area where Michelle and Linsk were sitting earlier. I hear Reeves say, "Where's Pilsen," as we get closer to the tables, and I respond, without even meaning to, out of habit I guess, "It's on the pink line." I walk up behind Michelle, put my arms around her neck, and give her a kiss on the cheek, "We'll take you out there one day, some cool spots in between the rats, the gentrification, and all the hipsters beginning to take the place over." I slide around Michelle and deposit myself in Jo's lap. She giggles at me.

CASE

"We'll take you out there one day, some cool spots in between the rats, the gentrification, and all the hipsters beginning to take the place over," Andrei says in response to Reeves.

I watch Ella come around the table to where Kaisa, Mercury, and I are sitting. She runs her hand through my hair like she has for years now. I smile and bob my head like a puppy seeking more and more attention. She smiles and chuckles before tapping Kaisa on the shoulder, and leaning down to give Mercury a firm, but gentle kiss on the lips. Linsk lights up the way Christmas trees do at the sight and I feel my heart swim. Mercury darts their eyes in the direction of Linsk, likely checking to see if the kiss was okay with them. They seem to like what they find because they then lean their head back and nuzzle against Ella's open hand and stomach. Mercury grabs Ella's hand and smiles like a child opening the best birthday present.

Smiling, Kaisa says, "Sometimes I miss that old apartment, we had a lot of good times there, maybe its nostalgia, but that place feels like a piece of us."

"I feel that way about Miami," Linsk and I say at almost exactly the same time. Reeves laughs so hard he almost falls over onto Jo and nudges Andrei sitting in Jo's lap. I watch him run his hand across the short hairs on his chin and start laughing again.

"I guess we know where to go for family vacations," Michelle says raising her coffee cup and pointing it at the ceiling as if we've reached a major conclusion.

"I'm not sure I'll be traveling with this lot all that much, self care and all that," Ella says sticking her tongue out at the rest of us, "But I do enjoy this family portrait, hold on for a second," she pulls out her phone and snaps a picture of the eight of us sitting around the two tables in the middle of the coffeeshop.

"That's just plain wrong," Jo says pulling out her own phone, "You have to be in it too Ella."

"I think it's prettier this way," Ella says laughing and ducking behind Mercury as Jo tries unsuccessfully to snap pictures of our side of the second table. Linsk is laughing on the other end, and we will later see a perfect snapshot where Jo caught them mid-laugh. Jo keeps taking photos of everyone and a cavalcade of funny faces get made alongside impromptu hugs and poses as the camera makes it way around the circle. Mercury stands up and Ella sits where they were sitting with Mercury now positioned in their lap. As if physically mirroring the reciprocity of the life they've built together over the years, Linsk jumped into Reeves' lap with a smile and Ella blew them a kiss. I turned to Kaisa and watched a small bit of moisture form in their eye as they watched the family laughing and hugging around the tables.

ELLA

I lose track of what Andrei is saying when I spot Mercury standing at the intersection down the block from New Wave.

I know exactly what they are doing. I would do the same thing. They are trying to decide whether or not to come meet the family. I want to run to them. I want to scoop them up in my arms the way Reeves bear hugs people. I want to tell them everything will be okay, that everyone here will love and care for them the way we all do for each other. I want to do each of these things, but instead, I sit and watch them at the intersection. I realize they have to make their own choices just like the rest of us did. I realize the types of healing that such autonomy can bring. Andrei stops talking and I light a smoke. I don't really want to smoke it, but I need something to do. I just watch them hoping they will take the leap, come on down the block, and see us. Behind the veils, the masks, the survival mechanisms, I can see a beautiful heart inside them just waiting to be set free, it reminds me of the rest of this little family. They fit here with us, maybe even more than I could put into words or explain to them or anyone else. I want to tell them this, but I just watch them as they make up their mind half a block away from me.

The sound of skateboards and the feeling of Andrei moving combine to take my gaze away from the intersection for a few moments. When I turn back, they're not there anymore. I don't know how or why, but I'm sure they decided to come to us. I just feel it inside. I pack up my bag, each thing going in the right space, each thing organized just so, and I look inside. I don't see them. I don't know if I could from this angle. I feel them, however, and somehow that tells me they are close. I'm trying to see through the window when Andrei's phone goes off beside me. I know what it says before he tells me. I ask him if he wants to go inside and say hello. We both know I'm going inside.

Inside, everything seems to be happening in the same moment. I see a picture of a fantasy wrapped within a dream that somehow seems to be coming true before my eyes. I watch the eight of them

135

laughing, talking, kissing, cuddling, and I take a photo to try to capture the moment for all eternity. Jo doesn't like me leaving myself out of photos. We fake argue about it all the time. She notices this time too and starts taking all kinds of photos herself. I hide behind Mercury and feel them laugh. They keep looking at Linsk, Reeves, and Case. They are making sure this is real. They are making sure it's okay to love and be loved. They are finding their place the same way each of us did within the chaotic cobwebs of this particular familial structure. I feel them sigh. I hear them snort in the midst of a powerful laugh. They beam. The smile seeks out the other ones around the table and Jo captures it more than once in her photos.

What could have been five minutes or fifteen hours later, Linsk and Reeves are headed home for some Netflix and wine. Case and Kaisa are heading off with Jo for some noodles at a place off the California stop they can't seem to get enough of in the past month. Michelle and Andrei are going for a walk and to listen to the music in the square tonight. I take Mercury's hand. They smile at me. I kiss them in a way that feels like rolling rapids finding the soft embrace of an expertly crafted river basin. We exit New Wave, and I ask if they are hungry. They smile and nod. Together, we walk down the street to Daisies because I'm in the mood for some pasta. Hand-in-hand, the sun gone for the day, we stand on the sidewalk in front of Daisies staring into each other's eyes.

REEVES

The view will take your breath away said the woman who sold me my tea at the Hyatt.

She was right. I stood on a rock looking out over the water. Early May 2018, I live in Chicago now, I said to myself staring at the ripples cascading in the glimmering sunshine. The rock was larger than it needed to be, to hold me that is, but it seemed fitting – the city seemed somehow bigger than it needed to be for me in the moment. I thought about Ella telling me about this place as we finished unpacking my stuff the night before. I smiled. She said she stayed here by accident a few years back when she was passing through the city. Case was new to the city. It was Ella's first time back since her dark days, as she called that period of intoxication and isolation we know as her twenties. She said she just picked a deal on one of those internet sites. She did not expect to find something magical she would return to over the years.

I took a sip of my tea and thought about the woman in the Hyatt. She had soft blonde streaks in her hair. I asked her about the view of the water. She said it was quite a hike to make it through the stairwells and hallways of McCormick Place, but she said it was worth it. She told me to enjoy the walk and gave me my tea in a large cup. Ella had warned me that I wouldn't likely find anywhere to grab a drink between the Hyatt and the waterfront. I enjoyed the walk through McCormick Place. I noticed the same places that sold food and drinks just as closed as Ella said they were damn near every time she walked through the place. I remembered Ella showing me a photo years ago of her and one of Linsk's co-workers posing by the no-longer-working pay phones in the belly of the massive structure. I followed the signs for restrooms when I was inside just so I could stand in the same spot.

Linsk was smiling, perched on the couch, paperback Ian Fleming novel in hand, as Ella told me about the place. They knew how much I liked to go out roaming on my first day living in a new place. Ella remembered from Miami. Linsk remembered from all my stories about doing so in different places. Ella picked this place because she loved to come here on days where she needed to think while visiting the city. She also picked the place because she brought Linsk here once when they visited the city. Linsk was attending an academic conference in Chicago and the conference was at the convention center. Linsk was overjoyed that a couple of co-workers with similar autoimmune conditions they located online came to the city to meet them and Ella. They spent three days with these co-workers having a blast. Case still raved about an Indian buffet they all fell in love with off the blue line near the Amtrak station. Ella brought them all here, and they sat out on rocks by the water.

I sat on the same rocks thinking about my new home. I remembered childhood train rides in New Jersey as I took the red line down to this part of town from the loop. I started in the loop having a welcome to the city breakfast with Ella and Linsk. We ate at a Corner Bakery Café beside the Palmer House where Linsk and Ella had breakfast when they were here for Linsk's conference. Ella was in love with the place, and often came here for coffee even though she said there were so many better independent coffee options nearby. We sipped our drinks and ate our breakfast without a lot of talking. It was just nice to be waking up and starting the day in the same city after the past year of adjustments and travel and packing and moving. The three of us were holding hands at about the same moment it hit me that the move was finally finished. We lived here now. I said that very loud into the water from my perch on the rock and let out a deep breath. Somehow, it felt like the water understood how I felt.

MICHELLE

"That's just the beginning of summer in the city," Jo said laughing as Mercury stared across the green expanse of the park at the people setting up for the concert.

"Yeah, once the weather gets nice, it's like a madhouse out here all the time," I said laughing and lighting a smoke. Jo was reading a paperback novel from a press based here in Chicago that had something to do with a mystery and some events in the 1960's. She had been talking about the book for weeks, but I wasn't paying nearly as much attention as she might have thought I was. The sun seemed brighter than just a few days ago. It always felt this way to me when the warm weather really took hold. I looked down at my still unopened Colson Whitehead novel that Ella said I would just love. Maybe I would start it today, maybe tomorrow, it wasn't important in either case. Ella was always suggesting books she thought I would love. I looked out across the park with a smile. Seven years in the city, and it still seemed like the air itself changed when the end of May came around each spring. There were kids playing in the grass. There were parents reading books and checking their phones with the occasional glance to make sure the children were still accounted for and not yet dead. There were people playing music and tourists who either sought out the park or got lost in it after a wrong turn in the loop, it was hard to tell the difference to tell you the truth, but they were certainly tourists.

"Classes are only a couple months away," Mercury said softly, as if speaking under their breath or maybe like they were afraid the words would bite them, "I should probably start getting ready for the fall at some point, right?"

"Relax," Jo said laughing and tossing her hair to the side, "That is months away, you should just keep enjoying the way Ella makes you giggle, that's the best kind of summer plan."

"I gotta agree with Jo here," I said smiling and flicking an ash.

"But don't you think Ella will be busy with her new novel or, I don't know, maybe moving on soon, I mean, we've been hanging out like all the time for months now," Mercury said and again, I swear, it sounded like they thought one of us would hit them for speaking. They ducked their head after they finished, and I watched them playing with the grass like a child bored or lost in the middle of a school day in some small town. I don't know why, but I felt the urge to hug them in that moment and tell them everything would be okay.

"Mercury," Jo said beating me to the punch, "You have to stop being so mean to yourself, Ella loves you, and for the record, so do we," she said pointing back and forth between the two of us. "Nobody is 'moving on' from you, you are family."

"Again," I say smiling, "I gotta agree with Jo, I mean, come on Mercury, if this family was going to get tired of anyone, don't you think Jo and I would already been kicked to the proverbial curb?"

Jo almost falls over laughing and says, "Well, damn Michelle."

"That is hard to argue with," Mercury says, and I notice their voice has its character, or maybe its shape, its strength, what makes a voice, I don't know, but Mercury's is back now. Mercury shoots a look I can only define as sarcastic at Jo and starts to laugh. Jo throws her book at Mercury and I can't help but chuckle as Mercury moves their arms just fast enough to swat it away. I flick another ash from my cigarette as some kid starts screaming about something, maybe ice cream, who knows, somewhere close to us in the park.

ANDREI

I remind myself for the seventeenth million time never to owe Ella a favor again as I walk up to the register at the Reckless Records in the loop.

It seemed like such a smart plan. There was no way it could be anything but easy. It was perfect. I would have Ella do some readings of texts that I wanted to weave into some of my beats. I would use poetry I had written in college. I would use research papers Michelle had written in her graduate program. I would use the poems Linsk let me have that they wrote to process what it was like to make peace with being an orphan. I would use the snippets of discarded ideas from Ella's journals and the little notes that Case left on the fridge that never seemed to contain a full thought even though Kaisa somehow understood them. I would use all these things for content. I would use Ella's sweet, sexy southern voice. This would be the perfect thing to weave in between the beats for the record I was making.

"Yes," I said to the sales clerk, Ron, who I sometimes saw at shows, "I would like to purchase these six albums." I could feel myself blushing. I could feel him judging me. I can't believe Ella made me do this. I bet she's dying laughing at the thought of it. I wouldn't be surprised if she wasn't even busy today, she's probably outside the store waiting to make fun of me as I exit in a few minutes. I will never owe her a favor again.

I should have just paid Ella to read the words into the recorder for the album. That's what I should have done. That's what I was going to do. That's what I had planned. I was going to do it, just pay her for her time, but no, Michelle had to point out that Ella would probably do it for free or for some favor or something like that. Michelle had to say that. Case had to agree. Jo had to call Ella. I had to be a cheapskate idiot. That's just what had to happen. And it had to go the way it did, it just had to. Ella had to say yes. Ella had to say she just needed a little favor in return, an errand she needed handled before her date with Mercury if I could swing it. Of course, I could swing it, that's just what

I had to say. I didn't even think to ask what the favor or the errand or the utter embarrassment, as it turned out, was, no, I didn't think of that.

"Little out of character for you," Ron says, and I just feel the laughter in his eyes. I knew right away that everyone in every club I ever played would know about this before the end of the day, probably before Ella's date with Mercury tonight now that I thought about it.

"They're for a friend," I said knowing that I wouldn't believe me if I was Ron.

"I'm sure they are," Ron said before telling me the price. Damn, I thought, they're also more expensive than they have any right to be, at least Ella's paying for them. Shit. Never owe Ella a favor again, never, not even one more time, not again.

I handed Ron the money. I cursed Ella's name for a few seconds thinking about just how much fun the guys at the clubs were going to have with this story over the next few weeks and maybe years. Nothing was more likely to leave a mark on your reputation as an edgy artist in the hipster crowds of today like people thinking you liked pop music. I could just see Ella laughing her ass off at me as I stood there in the record store, in the tourist part of town no less, wondering just how many jokes I would be the butt of due to this one event. Ron smiled at me. I smiled back while remaining aware of just how much he was enjoying my shame. He handed me the bag with each of the albums Taylor Swift had released on vinyl, and I grabbed it harder and faster than was probably necessary promising myself to get Ella back for sending me to pick these things up in the first place.

CASE

It's hard to describe the fear that cut through me like a sword in 2013.

The message was simple enough. It was only four words and an abbreviation. Hell, they were short words. I stared at the screen, the text message like a bad omen chilling my bones in an old school fantasy story. I stared at the phone. I read the words five times – "I NEED YOU HERE ASAP." Linsk was not the type to use capitalization to make a point. Linsk was not the type to need anyone or anything ASAP. What was going on, I wondered as I typed my own reply – "I can leave anytime, what's going on?" I forgot all about the interview transcripts on my lap. I forgot all about the Mexican take out I had ordered from the little family restaurant I loved a few blocks from the Jumping Bean. I forgot everything about my day-to-day life and all the little things I was supposed to be doing in the next few days. I feel like I forgot everything and just wanted to get to Linsk as fast as humanly possible – I guess that's exactly what happened.

"I'm booking you a ticket, check your email," Linsk messaged me back.

Was Linsk dying, my anxiety riddled brain screamed at me. What was going on? Linsk was supposed to be resting. They had fallen a week prior to this message. The fall had cracked their tailbone. They were supposed to be resting. Ella was taking care of them. The doctors had told Ella and Linsk that the pain would ease and there should be no lasting complications. Were there lasting complications now, I wondered? I texted Michelle and told her I needed someone to watch the rat's nest I lived in at the time. She said she had it covered. She didn't ask any questions. She knew I would fill her in on things. I knew Linsk would fill me in on things. What the hell was going on, why did I need to rush to the airport? I thought these things as I left my apartment less than fifty minutes after getting the message. I had a bag. I had my wallet. Michelle was on her way to the rat's nest. I had my flight information in my email on my phone. I closed the door and headed for the airport as the next text showed up on my screen.

"Ella has fucking disappeared, she just walked out on me, I don't know what's going on."

I thought about that trip in 2013 as I made my way to the apartment building I used to live in that was now Mercury's home on the last day of June 2018. I wasn't sure what to expect, but I was moving as fast as I could. Ella called right as Linsk texted me telling me to call Ella. It was around two in the morning. Ella told me that Jo called her terrified about Mercury right as my phone started going off in my ear. Jo was calling me as well. I got off the phone with Ella after agreeing to meet her at my old building and told Jo we were on it and would get Mercury home safely. Mercury was at the Driftwood on Montrose. It was a little bar that Ella called a tavern for no particular reason. It was a place Ella and Jo had each gone to get drinks with Mercury at some point. Ella sounded panicked, freaked out, scared. It reminded me of what Linsk's text messages felt like in 2013. "We all got to work out our shit," Kaisa said as I told them what was happening and where I was going in the middle of the night, "I guess it's Mercury's turn to realize they are actually important enough to hurt and scare us." I turned onto Clarendon at the so-familiar corner thinking that was exactly what this was.

We'd all been here before, so convinced we didn't deserve anything good that the appearance of good things sent us spiraling into a tunnel of darkness. I remembered pushing Ella against the wall at a beat-down karaoke bar in Miami. I remembered the shock in her eyes as she hit the wall. I remembered the sound her beer bottle made slapping her thigh. I remember how scared I was, even though I was doing the right thing damnit, that she would hate me. I remember it all too well. "What the fuck is wrong with you," I screamed at her, "What kind of piece of shit walks out on their sick partner, especially when they know that partner has been abandoned and alone like that before, what the hell Ella?"

"Have you ever considered that Linsk is probably much better off without me, I tend to screw up everything I touch if you haven't noticed?" Ella was shaking. She was crying. Her voice didn't even sound like her, it sounded like some scared child lost in a mall. She was pulling at her wrist, then she was pulling on her hair, she couldn't stay still. It was almost like she was trying to escape her own skin, like her own body was a trap of some sort. It reminded me of the way a child would struggle to get up after an ocean wave knocked them flat.

"Don't give me that, you know better than that, don't repeat your asshole abusers to me like it's not the piece of shit lie it's always been, what is your problem?" I remember clearly considering, for just a second, I'm not proud of it, it was just a second, taking it back, saying I was sorry, begging her not to hate me for screaming at her like that. I stood strong, it was hard, I didn't want to lose her, but I wanted to kill her at the same time for hurting Linsk. The look of utter sorrow on Linsk's face, that kept me going, that helped me scream.

"Can you stop yelling at me," Ella says trying with all her might not to look me in the eyes. She reached down to pull out her pack of cigarettes and I smacked them out of her hand. The pack fell onto the sidewalk in a jagged way, it sat there alone, like Linsk at home. Ella looks down at it. It's like something in the pack of cigarettes reminds her of herself, the worst parts of herself that had been tossed aside in gutters and against walls and anywhere that was out of the way throughout her life, I had to get her to look at me, look at right now, remember she wasn't the trash those jerks all convinced us we were at one time or another.

"Can you get your head out of your ass, you're scared, I get that, but when has running away or drinking so much you can't form words done you any good?"

The words ring in my head. I remember how angry and scared I felt. I remember Ella telling me she slept in a park the night before and how much I wanted to kill her for putting herself in danger. I remember we yelled for a while that night. She finally broke down and started crying even harder than she had been already. She only said she hated me fifteen times in the process. I remember the tears in Linsk's eyes before I left to go find Ella at whatever dive bar she was at. I knew she would be at one of them likely searching for cocaine or other forms of incidental suicide, anything to avoid feeling things and realizing she couldn't stand seeing Linsk in pain or considering life without them. I remember Ella, however much time after the first yelling, sitting on the concrete sobbing about how no one could love her, and she wasn't supposed to be happy. I remember cradling her in my arms, feeling the earlier dropped and now crushed pack of cigarettes beneath my own tailbone as I sat there rocking her back and forth.

I hit the button for Mercury's apartment number. The sound that I remembered so well screamed into the empty night and the door unlocked itself. It sounded like someone was having an argument in the parking lot of the gas station behind me on the other side of Clarendon. I walked up the familiar set of steps and got on the elevator on the right. I remembered often wondering when the day would come that I got stuck in one of these elevators that creaked like the knees of a perfect case of arthritis. Maybe tonight's the night, I thought and laughed at the possibility. Mercury was staying on the third floor. I got to their door and found Ella standing with it open. She looked at me, and said, "I need to go curse for a little while and maybe smoke four cartons of cigarettes, you got this?" I nodded moving past her into the apartment and taking a position on a stool beside the couch where Mercury was sleeping off however much alcohol they had tried to kill the pain with throughout the night.

LINSK

What the hell, I thought as the phone went off on the nightstand beside our bed.

I looked at the clock on the little brown table on the other side of the room. Two o'clock in the damn morning, who is calling us this late? Did Ella forget to put her phone on nighttime mode? It hit me then, was there an emergency? Ella always put her phone on nighttime mode, but each of the family numbers were in the favorites so those would ring no matter what. Was one of the family calling, I thought right as Ella sat up in bed and said, "Where are they," before moving out of the bed and beginning to put on clothes in a frenzied series of half-asleep movements that would have likely been hilarious under any other circumstances. I turned to my right, but Reeves was not moving. He was still asleep. How are you sleeping through this, I wondered and even thought about waking him up to ask, I'm too tired for this.

"What's going on," I asked from the middle of the bed. I was in the middle because tonight we decided, as we did sometimes, to sleep as a threesome. Reeves was somehow still asleep on my right as Ella frantically got dressed on my left. It was kind of a funny picture in my half-asleep mind. I could hear Jo's voice coming through the phone. She sounded worried, I could tell that even in my semi-consciousness. She was in Atlanta for some meeting with other alumni from Agnes Scott or maybe it was something else that I couldn't remember at the moment, but she was in Atlanta, of that I was sure. I wondered what could possibly be going on in Atlanta that necessitated Ella getting out of the bed and putting on clothes in a goofy dance, for lack of a better description, routine that I swore could have fit on a sitcom from the 1970's or 1980's. I imagined some canned eighties background music playing as she struggled with the clothes and started chuckling. I thought about waking up Reeves just for the hell of it.

Ella put down the phone, and said, "That was Jo, Mercury is shitfaced and talking about killing themselves at that tavern in uptown

147

we went to a while back. Jo said they're all alone, babbling about some girl that Jo has never heard of, and crying so hard that she can't really understand what they're trying to say other than that they're locked in the bathroom of the place and repeating that everyone hates them, and they don't deserve to live." Ella leans down, gives me a quick kiss, and says, "I'm going to go get them and take them home."

"Call me if you need me babe," I say as she disappears from the bedroom. She doesn't take her phone, which means she's still getting ready. Ella is never all that coordinated when she first wakes up, sometimes I wonder how she even manages to dress herself in the morning, but that's a question for another day, or another lifetime. Then, thinking about it as my mind is kind of starting to wake up and process what is going on, I say, "There is cash on the counter if you need it and I'll be up and headed there to if you need me to come or if you should stay here since you have that meeting in the morning?"

"Thanks love," Ella says swinging back into the room and picking up her phone. She has the cash in her hand, and adds, "But I'm not worried about the meeting, I'll call if I need anything," before heading back out the door moving as fast as she can. I want to go back to sleep. I feel Reeves wiggle his butt against me the way that always makes me smile. I still wonder if Ella taught him how to do that because of how much I love it. I'm not going back to sleep yet, I think, there is no way. I rub the spot on the bed where Ella was sleeping.

My eyes feel heavy, but not with sleep. I'm awake. I'm completely awake. I'm worried about Mercury. I'm remembering 2015 and 2013. I'm remembering when Ella slammed hard into her traumatic past and ran away from me certain that I would leave her sooner or later anyway. I feel the ache in my chest all these years later. I also smile at the work of Case back then to be there on the rare occasion where I really needed someone to come through for me. I grab my phone, and text case – "Call Ella right now!" Case was also there in 2015 when I walked out on Ella. Ella had just started making some real money from her writing, more than enough to just get by. There was a part of me that, somehow, thought that she was with me, at least partially, because I had resources that she did not. I thought the money would set her free, and I would be left behind. I couldn't see her wanting to stay with a sick orphan now that she had resources. I laugh now thinking about how Ella and Case hugging outside a bar made me, for just a moment, so jealous and scared that I woke up long enough to tell Ella how I felt.

The times that came after those two events were anything but easy. Ella and I worked through the trauma of her past and of mine. We relied on each other. We trusted each other – and Case – more than we had ever been willing to trust anyone else we had ever known. We cried a lot. We yelled a lot. It still hurts that she abandoned me when I was in so much pain. I know it still hurts her that I abandoned her too. It hurt so much, but the pain became kind of a security blanket of sorts for us. The pain evolved into this shared shield we carried with and for each other. We came out of the pain with armor that nothing could penetrate, we knew we could come through anything, we could climb any mountain together, we had proven it to ourselves along the way. It doesn't hurt the same anymore, it hurts, but more so, it is a reminder of just how lost and alone we felt before we found someone who was worth caring about before we figured out that the evil voices and deeds of our pasts did not get to define who we are and what we do.

I wonder if this will be a similar moment for Mercury, or maybe just the first big break down before the even bigger terrible moments come later. I wish I could take away their pain the same way I wish this with the rest of the family and even for myself. I know I can't. I know the healing, if they decide to keep going, will take its own shape. I know this, but I realize in the middle of this night that I'm ready to help them down the path the same way each of us has had to come out of the darkness as part of building this family. Mercury is family too, whether they can believe it or not yet, they are family and we'll take care of them like we do each other. I don't know what that will look like just yet, I admit to myself while holding Reeves and the stuffed koala bear Ella loves even tighter than usual. I don't know what their path will be, but I do know we are better than the world taught us to think we were and the pain is like a butterfly escaping from a cocoon, messy, terrible, but ultimately a beautiful rebirth that can lead to the most amazing and unexpected joy.

ELLA

The car cannot move fast enough through the deserted streets.

Jo said Mercury sounded like they were dying on the phone. I can feel my heart clench at even the thought. I think about the nights they wake up sweating and crying in their sleep. I think about the way they shake their clothes off to try to reduce the heat that builds in their skin in the midst of the nightmares. They talk about her in their sleep, but they never say who "her" is. I've tried to get them to talk about it when they're awake, but they haven't been ready yet. I watch the red light that seems to be taking an eternity to change. It's a fifteen minute drive, I tell myself, a fifteen minute drive. I keep repeating this. It helps, but then again, it doesn't. I have this image of getting to the bar too late. I have this image of cradling what used to be a living and breathing Mercury. I try to push the image away. I try to focus on anything else. I try to remain positive, isn't that what people say to do in these situations, it doesn't work.

My mind retreats to the many nights in my twenties when I was in the bathroom stall or the gutter, too much alcohol to feel my potential death, too much pain to care. My mind flashes to 2013 when I abandoned the only perfect person I had ever met after they were injured because I was scared no one could ever love me, and they would leave me someday anyhow. It was stupid. It made no sense. It was wrong. So were the nights where I was Mercury in this or that bar, city, train station, truck stop, or stranger's bed. My mind flashes to 2015 when I got a taste of my own medicine, when I was the one abandoned without any clue what to do and for once having chosen to stay once I got the chance again after my own screw ups. An image of Mercury sleeping peacefully flutters in my eyes alongside an image of them being attacked, like I was so many times in so many bars, dances right beside it. I scream and scare the driver.

The car finally arrives at the bar, and I jump out much faster than the driver is likely happy with. He was trying to talk to me, I was trying to find Mercury. I make my way through the door past a bouncer who seems to be able to tell I'm in a hurry. The music is loud, a song by a band I don't recognize that for some reason involves screaming in anguish, I get that. I can't shake the images from my head as I push through the crowd as last call is reaching its climax. I get to the bathrooms and there are people outside of them. Some folks are yelling into one of them saying it's been closed for too long. I call Mercury's name. It might be twenty seconds. It might be hours. The door cracks open. Mercury asks me what I'm doing there. I tell them I came to take them home. They smile, eyes glazed like the ones you see on dead bodies in the morgue before they are prepared for a funeral, don't ask me how I know that. They say they're fine. They say they're going to sleep. I pick them up.

The driver didn't wait like I asked him to. Of course, he didn't. I flag a cab. It comes to the curb and I put us both in the car. My mind goes to a small room in this city where Kaisa is crying about a smaller room where they hid from the violence of childhood. My mind visits a three-month period where Case wouldn't speak to me because an abuser convinced them I was a problem whenever I sought to get them out of that situation. My mind recalls Andrei screaming at the water, anguish sketching his face, as he recalls being sexually assaulted in high school. My mind sneaks into a funeral home where Michelle falls to the floor shaking as memories of her mother's funeral flood her body on a Tuesday. My mind beckons me with images of Reeves heaving and sobbing at childhood ghosts that came to torture him on a stormy night in Miami when sleep was his worst enemy. The car pulls up in front of the building Case used to live in on the corner of Lawrence and Clarendon.

Mercury says they love the Taylor Swift albums as I pull their keys from the side pocket in the bag they carry everywhere. Mercury tells me I'm going to leave them and that I don't love them as I use the fob on the keychain to open the outer door to the building. Mercury slurs something about a highway, a girl, and a scream as I hit the button for the elevator. Mercury says I'm too good for them and that I'm an asshole as the elevator doors open. Mercury begs me not to hurt them and covers their face as I open the door to their apartment and the smell of alcohol hits me in the face. Mercury says please don't leave me and that its all their fault as I put them on their couch, wipe off pieces of leftover vomit from their chin, and put a blanket over their athletic frame. I pull a stool from the side of the room. I sit on it. I watch Mercury as they finish passing out on the couch and wait for Case to arrive so I can take a little walk to clear my nerves and try to get the images of terrible things happening to Mercury and the rest of my family out of my head.

MERCURY

It takes me a few minutes to figure out where I am when I wake up on the first day of July.

My eyes hurt. My head hurts. My throat hurts. Everything hurts. I recognize the two tiny end tables I put together as a coffee table. I'm in my apartment. I don't know how I got here. I'm still wearing the clothes I was wearing when I left the house last night. I don't remember why I left the house. I went to sleep at seven, but I woke up at some point. She was in my dreams again, but this time, Ella was there too, and they were both leaving me. I'm still in the same clothes. Did I go somewhere? I think I did. I left the house, I remember that. I run my hands down my body. My own touch is painful. The sunlight is too bright. My tank top feels like it spent some time in a garbage can while I slept. I take off the clothes. I need them, ugh, gone. I throw them on the floor and try to remember.

I stand up because I need some water. Standing up was a mistake. My head swims and I have to sit back down. I hear the scream on the highway. I try to push it from my mind, but I can't, I'm too tired. I'm awake, but it's here in the waking morning light now, just like it comes in my dreams at night. I can see her. She's standing in the middle of the highway. She's watching the taillights fade away into the darkness. She screams after the car. She wants it to come back. She tries to run after the car. She thinks this can't be real. She thinks she is dreaming. She runs down the deserted road. She falls. She skins her knees. She cries. She screams with everything she has. Nothing. There is no sound. It's just her, the road, and the night. She feels the pain in her knees. She tries to get off the road. She makes it to the side, the same side the car stopped on when she was inside it. She falls down. She sleeps.

I get a glass of water. I go to the bathroom. What happened last night? I don't know. I kind of remember calling Jo. I think I wanted to talk to Jo. I was going to call Ella. Ella hates me, I remember thinking, but I don't remember why I thought that. I move around the apartment.

Everything seems normal except there is stool beside the couch. I move it back to the side of the room, by the window, where it belongs. That is when I hear a noise and look up. My bed. There is someone in my bed. It is so high up, raised above like an old-time bunkbed so I could use the space underneath it for storage. I got it from some girl named Mattie that was moving out of the building the day I moved into this apartment. Mattie said her dad built it for her when she came to Chicago for graduate school years ago. I wondered what it was like to have parents that would build you a bed or do anything for you really.

There is blood in the car before it stops on the side of the road. I don't want to see this, but she's back in my head. There is blood in the car. It's on the dashboard. There is a bag on the dashboard beside the blood. She's hungry. She knows not to say this out loud. She knows they won't want to hear this. She knows they'll get mad. There is nothing out here. The car stops on the side of the road. They are doing something in the front seat. She can't see what they are doing. She knows better than to ask. She knows better than to make sounds. Her nails hurt when she accidentally touches her leg in the backseat while they are doing something in the front seat. They are raw, she bites them when it feels too hard to do anything else. She wonders where they are. All she can see are fields full of peanuts. She doesn't know what peanuts taste like yet. She'll learn that later. They tell her to get out of the car. One of them does too. She doesn't want to get out of the car. She knows better than to say this. She knows she must obey. She gets out of the car and stands by the one who already got out of the car. I don't want to think about this. I don't want this dream or memory or whatever it is.

I check my bed. Ella is sleeping in it. She looks peaceful. What is she doing here? I check my phone. I didn't call her. I called Jo. Did Jo call Ella? Did I go to see her? What is she doing in my bed? I want to touch her. I'm scared to do it. Why am I scared to touch Ella? I need more water. My arms shake, and I pick at them the way I did when I was little. I don't know why. I didn't know why back then either. I walk over to the window. The sunlight is filling the open space behind the building. I stare at it. She tries to come back into my mind, but I'm able to push her out now. I'm waking up, I think, I'm not sure why I think this or why it feels like both happy and sad news at the same time. I start humming a song as I watch the sun in the empty lot behind the building. I don't know what song it is. I'm waking up, I think again, but again, I don't really know what I mean by this. The sun hurts my eyes.

TWITTER BOY

I am more than a little freaked out when I think of Jo's family. Okay, I'm even more than more than a little freaked out.

I'm not even sure I can keep all the names straight. Ella is the writer. Linsk is the medical researcher. Reeves is the artist. Case is the graduate student who is really a painter. Kaisa helps marginalized kids. Mercury is the new one who scared Jo the other night, they are going to graduate school for something about health. That's right. That's it. Is that right? Who did Jo meet first? Jo met Mercury first, wait then how is Mercury the new one? Wait, that's it. Mercury and Jo went to college together, but then Jo met Ella and maybe Mercury did too, when they were in college, maybe is that right, that might be right, shit, okay, let me think. Okay, whew, deep breath, okay, Jo met Mercury in college then Ella gave a talk at the college. Yeah, that's it. Okay So, Mercury is not new to Jo but new to the family. And Jo is the other new one, is that right? She talks about them like she's known them forever, how am I supposed to keep all this straight? Okay, deep breath, I can do this, Jo is worth this anxiety, okay, that much I know.

Okay, Jo met Case and Kaisa when she came to Chicago. Right, yeah, that's right, okay, that's right, I got this. This family won't even fit into a tweet, what the hell is that? Okay, so then through Case and Kaisa, here in Chicago, yeah, through them Jo started hanging out with Ella, like more informally, not just meeting them at a book talk, okay, got it. That went on for a while, and they saw something special in Jo, who wouldn't see something special in Jo? Obviously, everyone does, they just have to, don't they, okay. So, then Jo was invited to a family gathering, was that it, yeah, it was for some holiday. They met Linsk and Reeves then, but Linsk and Reeves already knew Case and Kaisa, but did they know Mercury yet? Maybe, I don't know. I don't think so. Maybe Linsk did. Yeah, I think Jo said Linsk did. Okay.

So, then they all moved to Chicago, but where do Andrei and Michelle come in? How do I keep this all straight? What if these people hate me? I love Jo, but what if this family portrait of love she's found see me and tell her to run the other way. What if I get Ella mixed up with Michelle, they both have beautiful hair, that's what Jo says, okay, wait, take a breath, you're losing your shit man, calm the fuck down! Okay, so Michelle is friends, or was friends but I guess still is because friends are family and family are friends, yeah, so Michelle gets to know Case in graduate school before Michelle leaves to work in nonprofits, for women's reproductive health, I'm sure that's it. Andrei is with Michelle and they love each other in the more than friends kind of way like I love Jo and Jo loves me, I hope Jo loves me, damn!

Okay, I got this. The family is all nine of them, ten with me, right? Yeah, that's the hope. I mean, it would be nice to have a family, but damn that's intimidating, all these people love and care for Jo, I gotta get this right. Okay, the family is the nine of them. Linsk, Ella, Reeves, and Mercury are one romantic unit of sorts – Linsk and Reeves, Linsk and Ella, Ella and Mercury, okay got it. Then, Case and Kaisa are a unit. Okay, got that, and Michelle and Andrei are a unit. Okay, I think that's right, and then they all pull together, I guess like really close siblings or parents or what not for Jo and for each other, yeah, that's right, okay, I think I got it. Maybe I should make flash cards or something like that. Do they still sell flash cards in the age of computers, is that still a thing, if so, maybe I should do that?

Okay, you got this man, you got this. Okay, only two weeks. Two weeks from now will be the beginning of August. Two weeks before my next visit, the last one before I move to the city to be with Jo. Two weeks until I meet this family. Two weeks, I really do need to keep practicing, what if I say the wrong thing? What if I do something stupid? What if they all hate me and Jo doesn't look at me the same after that? Okay, calm down man, calm down, it will be fine, they love Jo and Jo loves me, so it'll be cool. Does Jo love me? I hope she does, damn anxiety, maybe I could meet them one at a time, maybe that would be easier, I should ask Jo about that, but what if she thinks I'm a coward? I don't know what to do, damnit. Okay, I got this, two weeks, that's plenty of time to get ready.

JO

"I know, I know, I'm sorry I scared you," Mercury says sitting on my bed on the third of July.

"That's not good enough, what the hell were you thinking," I almost hiss at them. I've never been so mad. They could have killed themselves or gotten assaulted or who the hell knows. "You can't just go nuclear on yourself like that, you scared the shit out of me!" I almost pull back when I see how their face changes. Tears start coming from their eyes, small droplets like the beginning of a summer rain. I want to hug them and tell them everything will be okay. I want to just rub their head and tell them we'll figure it out. I want to do these things, but before I can, I have to let out the fear running through my veins at the thought of them dying on the floor beside some toilet. The image haunts me and has ever since getting that call in the middle of the night at the end of June.

Crying even harder now, Mercury says, "I'm sorry, please don't hate me," and I watch their whole body shake. Violent shivers seem to erupt from their toes all the way up to their eyes. They are rocking back and forth, "Please don't leave me," they half-whisper, half-scream, "I'm so sorry, please don't hit me, please, please, please," their voice gives out on them and they just begin sobbing into their hands. I watch as their body continues to shake, sometimes faster and sometimes slower, until I wrap them in my arms, my anger and fear still boiling but slipping to the backburner for a few moments. I rub their head softly as it rests on my chest.

"I'm not going to hate you, leave you, or hit you Mercury," I say in the softest yet firmest voice I can mobilize, "I love you, that's why the thought of you dying on the floor of a bathroom in some strange place when I'm in another city terrifies me so damn much, you just can't do that kind of thing and not expect me to have a reaction, you just can't, that's part of loving you, I don't want you to hurt or be hurt by anyone, even yourself." I somehow manage to hold them even closer as a fresh round of sobs moves through their body. Images of them the way Ella described finding them in that bathroom flash through my mind. I wonder if I'll have to see these images again in the future. I know, somehow, that I'll see them anytime we're in separate cities again. I know that I'll see them anytime I find out they are drinking alone again. I know that I'll see them anytime they begin to feel distant. I don't want these images. I don't want to imagine life without my friend, life after a night like that goes as bad as it could have.

KAISA

"May I come in," I asked as Mercury answered the door on the seventh of July.

"I guess so," Mercury said. Their eyes were red. They moved from the doorway. I walked past them. I noticed right away that the apartment was spotless. It looked like they had been cleaning constantly. I had been planning this visit since talking to Jo at the family get together on the Fourth of July. Everyone noticed that Mercury did not come to the cookout. Everyone could tell how sad Ella was. Jo told me she had talked with Mercury in her apartment when she got back from Atlanta. She told me Mercury was struggling, sure that she wasn't good enough for Ella or the family. I remembered that feeling. I didn't spend time trying to die through an alcohol induced coma on a bathroom floor, but I did my fair share of other things in bathrooms that could have, maybe should have, killed me. I watched Case and Linsk watching Ella all day. I knew the scared looks they wore. I decided to try to see if I could get through to the newest family member the way Linsk got through to me.

"We missed you at the cookout," I said walking further into the apartment. I saw the metal stool that Case said Ella was sitting on when they got to the apartment that night. I looked at the stack of medical books and journals on the makeshift desk in the corner. Mercury came in behind me. They didn't say anything. They just sat on the couch and wrapped themselves in an Atlanta Braves blanket. They picked up a stuffed crow Ella got for them, and cradled it in their arms, holding it with enough force to make their fingers strain.

"I wasn't feeling well," they finally said.

"I bet you don't feel well a lot," I said pulling out one of the two small tables they had pushed together as a type of coffee table in front of the couch. I sat down on it, and continued, "In fact, I bet you often feel horrible, about yourself and about everything without being able to tell exactly why, sound about right?" I watched their eyes. The eyes don't lie, Ella always said. I saw recognition. "You don't have to tell me anything or talk about it, but I wanted you to know that I understand, and so does the rest of this family, we've all been through hell to get here." Their eyes were staring into mine, it was like they were looking for some kind of lie inside me that would make it okay to ignore what I was saying. I knew that look too. "I don't know who hurt you," I continued, "But I do know that it wasn't your fault and that you deserve better than however terrible you had to feel to end up on that bathroom floor."

They shook a little bit, squeezed the stuffed animal even tighter, and turned their eyes away from mine. "I know you don't believe me, but it's true," I said. "I spent some time on bathroom floors myself," I added, and they looked at me with eyes that were half-cold and half on the verge of tears. "I bet you had to create a mask, you had to push it all down, you had to hang on as tight as you could to survive, I bet you're exhausted, I know I was." They shook their head, but the movement was weak, slow, as if they were trying too hard to create the reaction they believed they should have. "I understand, it's terrifying to trust anyone after you've been really hurt, I know, I really do, but I also know that it can be more than worth it with the right people, I didn't know that once, but I do now."

I watched as they shrunk into themselves. I wanted to hold them, but I needed to see if I could reach them. I said, "Look, you don't have to do anything today, but," and here I paused as they turned to look at me, "You have to understand that the longer you try to hold it all inside, turn to bars and bathrooms rather than the people around you, or continue to believe the bad things others have said instead of the good things in your life now, the more you are likely to hurt Ella and the rest of us." I paused again. I could see them shaking their head. I could see their eyes trying to ignore what I said.

"I understand Mercury," I said pulling their eyes back to me at the sound of their name, "You don't realize or believe you can hurt us, but look around, you already did that once and you can again because we already love you." I watched them try to somehow shrink even more, and added, "You can keep doing the same thing and see just how much hurt we can take, or at some point, if you're willing and you really want a family who will love you the way you deserve, you can try to open up instead." I patted them on the knee as fresh tears came running down their cheeks. It was hard to see just how much like me they looked as I stood up. "It's up to you," I said. They didn't speak. I didn't think they would. I started moving toward the door, looking back with each step, and then I was out in the hallway, they were in their apartment. I wondered what would happen next.

ELLA

I could just make out Mercury standing by the window when I woke up on the first of July.

It wasn't until that moment that I realized I wasn't sure if they would wake up at all. It wasn't until that moment that I felt just how dirty I was after not having a shower for over twenty-four hours. It wasn't until that moment that I realized how tired I felt deep down in my bones after only falling asleep, according to the time on my phone, about three hours before I woke up in a bed I had only slept in with Mercury until that morning. It wasn't until that moment that I wondered if I had been right to send Case home after I got back from my walk around the block and after venting to them for a while as Mercury slept. It wasn't until that moment that I noticed the dried blood on my knuckle from punching the wall of the building while I was cursing, smoking, and crying on the sidewalk.

I sat up in bed. Mercury turned around at the sound. I remembered holding them in this bed just a few mornings before as they pushed their head against my chest and giggled. I remembered lifting them up into this bed multiple times as our lips remained connected in an embrace that now felt like something from another lifetime. I remembered them waking up in the middle of the night sweating and shedding their clothes and how they said it was fine and they didn't know what to say about it. I remembered they said it was just nightmares, that they were fine, and that I let it go even though I wasn't likely to do so again. I remembered my own nights on bathroom floors, bent over strange toilets, and making other people worry, cry, and scream as I tried to destroy myself. I remembered just how angry I wanted to be with them, but looking at them in the window, I just wanted to cry.

"Hey," they said with a sheepish look on their face, "I don't really remember much from last night, but I understand if you need to, you know, not see me anymore."

"Is that what last night was about Mercury," I asked looking at them as I began to move out of the bed, "You trying to run me off, because if you want me gone, just say so."

"I don't want you gone," they said and started crying. Their body started shivering the way they do whenever they become overwhelmed with emotion. I wanted to run to them, to hold them, but I couldn't. All I could think about is what it would have been like to wake up this morning and learn that they died on the floor of a bathroom in Uptown. I got off the bed. I stood in front of them. They continued to cry. "I don't know why you put up with me," they sobbed into the window as they turned their back on me, "You're just going to leave me, everybody leaves me, and it's all my fault, so why don't you just go."

"I don't know who everybody is Mercury, but I'm not them. I love you, and I have no desire to leave you," I said softly. It was simply the truth. The week before, we were talking about a future together. The week before, we were looking at potential apartments we could share together. The week before, we were talking about commitment to each other. The week before, I was imagining a future with this amazing, person I had somehow found that added things to my life, to Linsk's and Reeves' lives, to the family, that I didn't even know were missing until they showed up via a move to Chicago. It was hard to take any of that seriously, to really consider planning anything, when last night suggested they might be gone any minute, they might not be around for a future together no matter what they said. I felt a sickening sadness as I tried to cling to the dreams of last week at the same time that images of them in the bathroom at the bar, of them in a casket, of them gone flooded my mind. "I used to hate myself too," I say with my own sheepish look, "I don't know why you do, but if you want to talk about it, I'm here for you, I love you even if you don't love yourself yet."

I watched as they turned back to face me. Tears decorated their eyes like rainwater fitted to the exterior of a glass door. They tried to talk, but their voice caught in their throat. I wondered what they were going to say, maybe their usual I appreciate you, the closest they came to saying they loved me even though I was pretty sure they did love me. Pretty sure was the best you could do when someone you loved was always holding back, something I knew from the years where pretty sure was the best anyone ever got from me. They tried to speak again. Nothing came out. They began to sway, and I finally felt safe enough to reach for them. I wrapped them in my arms, they began to cry again, and I just held them.

LINSK

Ella barely spoke when she arrived at the house.

It had been over twelve hours since she left. I knew from text messages in the middle of the night that Mercury got home safe. I knew from text messages a couple hours earlier that Ella went roaming through the city to think. I knew from experience that roaming through the city likely involved a stop at Pizano's and Stan's on the way home. I watched her drop her keys and other essentials in the yellow bowl we kept beside the front door. I felt her peck me on the cheek as she made her way to the bedroom. I saw the worry on Reeves' face at her silence. He was sitting on the couch reading reports in preparation for some work at the new gallery. I heard Ella fall onto the bed in the master bedroom. I felt a sense of relief having her home. I felt a sense of deep sadness because I knew how much pain she was in after the previous night.

My mind returned to a different time and place. Collette was still living in Florida. It was when Ella and Collette were friends after they divorced. It was also after the abusive relationship Collette got trapped in right after her and Ella parted ways. Collette was back in Miami putting her life back together and dealing with the fallout from the abusive relationship. We were helping her. An old crush that had never treated her like a person in the first place, based on the stories she told Ella, came into Naples, Florida on vacation. He wanted to see Collette. She wanted to go see him. Ella didn't think it was the best idea. Collette said she would just drive up for a few hours, see him, and come back home.

Reeves leaves for his meeting after checking six times to make sure I don't need him to stay. I sit at my computer. Ella is still in our room. I checked on her a few times throughout the afternoon and early evening. She was sleeping the whole time. I can hear her moving from time to time, but she just goes back to sleep and never comes out of the room. I know this Ella. She is depressed. She is seeing flashbacks of all the death and violence from her life. She is imagining all those terrible things happening to Mercury. These images will plague her. She will handle it, but it will take a toll on her. I open a word document on my computer. I want to send Mercury a letter. I want them to know they're not alone. I want them to know that we are here for them, that we care, and that we've all had our terrible nights.

Collette texted in the evening from Naples. She had decided to stay the night. She had initially planned to meet up with Ella when she got back that night. She didn't mention this in her texts. Ella was used to being blown off by people, but it still hurt. We didn't hear any more from Collette until the middle of the night. She texted from a club called Dimension. She was drinking despite not mentioning she planned to drink that night earlier in any texts. She was out drinking with the old crush who never treated her like a person and his friend. As she always did when she was in trouble, she said she was "fine." Ella called her. I offered to drive out to Naples to get her, to bring her home safe. Ella offered this to her as well. Ella was too tired to drive anywhere, but she was still going to try to drive out herself if Collette said so.

I write Mercury a letter. In the middle of it, Ella comes out of the bedroom. Her eyes are bloodshot as if she hasn't slept at all. I know it's the nightmares. They are back again. She sees the people from the past in her dreams. I can tell the ghosts are back. She doesn't speak. She knows she doesn't need to. I smile at her. She walks out on the porch but stops to make a cup of coffee first. I hear the sounds of music. It sounds like sad songs. I know she's out there trying to make the images stop. I know there is nothing I can do. I know she loves Mercury. I know that means that there is no way to avoid this type of reaction to the thought of Mercury being hurt.

Ella would go outside to talk to Collette, but before she did, I could hear Collette on the other end of the phone. She was so drunk she could not properly say her own name. Her words were jumbling together as if she had taken some kind of speed or poppers or had some snuck into her drink. She sounded completely unlike herself and angry beyond words. I saw the tear rolling down Ella's cheek as she told me she was going outside to talk to Collette who had reluctantly agreed to get out of the club. I could see the pain in Ella's legs, it was a bad day for her body already. She was gone for hours. I fell asleep. I woke up again. When Ella came back, I could hear the sadness in her voice. In the morning, I could tell she hadn't slept at all. She stayed up worried about Collette.

I wondered if Ella would get to sleep anytime soon as I sent the email to Mercury.

CASE

I didn't want them to, but I felt my blood and my eyes go cold as I opened the door.

Mercury was standing there looking like they were ready for a firing squad. I'm not proud of the fact that it felt good to see them looking so worried. I wanted to tell Ella to never see them again after watching her look so sad for the past two weeks. Ella's new novel was in the trash, forgotten, lost, just gone. She was just sleeping and roaming around the city. She kept staring at bars, probably remembering Mercury's body on a bathroom floor or the days when Ella would have drowned her own pain and likely had to be found on her own bathroom floor. She was barely speaking. She was crying a lot. She was sharing text messages here and there with Mercury, but the two had not been in the same physical space since the morning after I had to go out to my old apartment in the middle of the night.

I considered not letting them in, but I knew that was the wrong thing to do. Ella loved them, and as much I wanted to protect Ella, I loved them too and so did Kaisa and Jo. Mercury knew we were doing a movie night. They were part of these before that night. They were always invited. Hell, Kaisa might have even reminded them of the this when they went for their visit last week. I moved aside. They walked past me into the apartment. I watched them from behind as they moved through the foyer and into the living room where the others were sitting. I felt an odd pull in my chest. I wanted to help Mercury, but I wanted to protect Ella from them at the same time. I remembered how I felt after I hurt Ella by turning my back on her when I got stuck in an abusive relationship. I wondered if she felt like I did tonight when I came running to her for help once I finally figured out how toxic that relationship was for me.

I walked into the living room as Mercury said, "I need to tell all of you something, especially Ella," before beginning to shake and cry. Kaisa stood up. Ella did too. Jo remained on the couch though her legs moved as if she was about to get up as well. Kaisa led Mercury over to one of the chairs by the television. They motioned for Ella and me to sit back down on the couch. They sat in front of Mercury on the floor. The cats came by, one perched on Kaisa and the other two joined Mercury in the chair. Mercury rubbed their arms as if giving themselves a fast hug. They exhaled a loud sigh, and said, "First, I'm sorry I've been so distant."

There were nods all around the room. Nobody spoke, nobody moved – we all watched Mercury and Kaisa sitting on the floor in front of them. Ella was shaking beside me. Kaisa was smiling. Jo was moving her head back and forth trying to watch, or maybe just protect, both Mercury and Ella at the same time. I could see the Chicago skyline through the window over Mercury's head. I watched the sky. I thought about the strength it had to take for Mercury to be sitting in this apartment, in front of us, looking like they would literally rather be anywhere else in the world. I wondered what the past couple weeks had been like for them. Ella believed in them. Linsk, Jo, and Kaisa did too. When I pulled off my obsessive-desire-to-protect-Ella-from-anything-bad-blinders for a few minutes, I realized I did too.

The other day over breakfast at the Growling Rabbit, Michelle pointed out that each of us had went through our own, as she put it, "clusterfucks" as we worked through trauma early into our times with this family. I could almost see both Reeves and Andrei nodding over their breakfast plates. I nodded the same way they did, sitting my toast down for a moment as the cars moved up and down North Broadway, and in my living room watching the sky above where Mercury was sitting, I hoped this was just their turn to start healing.

MERCURY

"I need to tell all of you something, especially Ella," I said sitting on a chair in Case and Kaisa's house on the fifteenth of July.

I had spent almost two weeks preparing for this moment, deciding to do it. I made myself stare at Ella. It hurt so much to look at her. She looked like she was braced for an attack. I noticed the suspicion written all over Case's face when they answered the door. Ella wasn't suspicious. She was sad. She was hurting. She was worried about me. I scared her. She should have been angry. She should hate me. She didn't. She was just worried about me. I just wanted to hold her, but I knew that if I touched her, I wouldn't be able to speak. I could feel Kaisa sitting on the floor in front of me. I could feel the cats moving around me, purring softly. I was so cold. I kept trying to use my hands to warm the rest of me. It wasn't working. The room felt large and small at the same time, everything seemed cloudy and scary and off. I took a deep breath, and said, "First, I'm sorry I've been so distant the past two weeks."

They all nodded. I thought about the mornings, afternoons, and evenings in my apartment over the past two weeks. I had been alone, mostly taking care of myself, for years, but for the first time, I really felt alone in my apartment after Ella left that morning. I thought it was over. I thought we were done. I was amazed when she texted me a couple days later. She just said she loved me and was available when I was ready to talk. It took me almost twelve hours to text her back. We had been texting since. I was even more surprised when Kaisa showed up. How did they know everything I was feeling; how did Ella know? The only answer I could come up with was that maybe they were just being honest, maybe they had felt the way I do now at some point in the past. Maybe they really did understand, if that was true, maybe they really did love me. Maybe someone could love me, I said to myself in the shower, in bed, on the couch. I just kept repeating it, hoping against hope it might be true, allowing myself to hope, to believe, to trust them instead of all the people from the past, all the ones who said I was difficult or wrong.

"I've been thinking about a little girl that I dream about a lot of nights," I said realizing this was not what I had planned to say. I had planned to apologize, to promise to do better, to say something that might placate them, buy myself some more time to figure things out. I didn't plan to tell the truth, but it just came out. "She is scared, and she has been beaten and abused her whole childhood. She is in the car with the people who are supposed to be her family. They are driving on a road in the middle of nowhere in Georgia." I didn't know how I was saying all this out loud. I didn't understand what was coming out of my mouth fully at the time. I wanted to stop, to pull it back, but I kept going, "The people who are supposed to be her parents are fighting again. They are drunk or maybe that's just how they seem to her. There is blood in the car from their most recent fight. They scare her, but she knows to be quiet."

It feels like the tears running down my face belong to someone else. I can feel them. I can even taste the ones that come to my lips, but they don't feel like my own. It's like my body is on autopilot, finally spilling out or throwing up the poison that has been living inside me for so long. "I can see her when I close my eyes. They stop on the side of the road. She has to get out of the car. There is no question, one of the people who is supposed to be her parent tells her to get out of the car. She knows that bruises always show up if she tries to say no, say anything." I wonder, for just a moment, how long I've been quiet, why saying what I feel is so much scarier to me than almost anything else. I'm guessing it started in that car, or maybe it started in the house where that car was parked before that ride in the middle of nowhere. "She gets out of the car. The supposed to be parent tells her to look at the pretty flowers. There are no flowers. She looks and looks, but there are only weeds on the side of the road and peanuts beyond the edge of the road. She looks anyway, she doesn't want to get bruised again, so she looks." I can see the images in my head as I speak. It's like I'm reading from a teleprompter like the people on CNN do with the news. I can almost smell the peanuts and feel the road beneath my feet.

I'm quiet for what seems like an eternity, but none of them move. Ella is looking at me with tears in her eyes. There is something soft, welcoming, or maybe just understanding in her eyes. Case is holding one of her hands. Jo is holding the other. They are both crying as well. I can't see Kaisa's face, looking down makes my own vision blurry because my eyes are like buckets under a leaky roof, filled with water that has nowhere else to go. "She watches as the car drives away from her. She watches the taillights. She screams at the car. She runs after it. She falls at some point. The car is gone. She skins her knees. She doesn't understand. She doesn't know what is happening. She never sees the people who are supposed to be her parents again. She gets picked up much later, after dark, by someone in a truck. The person in the truck takes her into a town nearby." It is the most I've spoken in years. I realize that as I speak. I wonder where my voice went and how I found it again. I don't know, I still don't know.

I take a deep breath. I let it out. I take another breath. I let it out. I notice that Ella is wearing a shirt I bought her when we were hanging out on the southside near the University of Chicago. I stare at the shirt, and continue, "She spends the next decade or so bouncing from place to place. She doesn't have a family. She doesn't understand what it means to have a home. She bounces and bounces and bounces. Some of the places are nice, at first, but she always had to leave, or they just leave her all alone again. Some of the places are horrible, and even thinking about them makes her sick. There are more bruises. There is more blood. There are many more supposed to be parents fighting. She is told she is too much trouble. She is told she is disgusting. She is told she is wrong, always wrong. She gets used to waiting for everyone to leave. That is what she thinks life is, waiting for people to leave when they get sick of her." I put my head down. I don't know what I'm saying anymore. I'm just word vomiting everything I feel.

I shake as sobs louder than a bear's cries escape my body. I shake harder and harder. Kaisa puts their hand on my knee. Ella jumps off the couch, but I hold up my hand. She stops. She stays there, standing in front of me with those soft, loving eyes. I need to continue. I think about the email Linsk sent me. I try to be strong, like they said, just strong enough, one moment at a time. I continue and, if I'm being honest with you, I say something I haven't been willing to admit for so long it feels like forever, "That girl was me."

I can't believe I said it. As sobs leave my body, I continue too terrified that I'll lose the strength to speak if what I feel doesn't get out of me right that moment, "I was her before I became me. It was before a transformed or transitioned into the me you all know. I left the homes with the supposed be parents when I was eighteen, I went to college, and I never looked back. I kept trying to outrun the dreams. I kept trying to leave that little girl behind. I didn't know how to handle all of you coming into my life, I thought if I showed you how messed up I was you would all run for the hills like everyone else, but you're still here." I feel my cheeks puff up with more tears flowing down my face, their own little rivers. I didn't know my body could hold so much water. "I'm so sorry, I'm so sorry, I don't want to leave, I want to stay with you, I want to be with Ella and be part of this family, please don't leave me," I say, and my voice feels like a hoarse scream in an empty night devoid of stars.

It happens faster than I could have imagined. I'm in Ella's arms. I'm crying so hard I swear my body will fall apart. Case is rubbing my back and telling me I'm home now. Jo is on the other side of me with Kaisa and they're both reaching for me. Ella rubs my head, holds me tighter than my own chest feels, and whispers in my ear, "I got you, you're safe now, I won't leave you, we won't leave you, we love you." I don't know how many times she says this. I can feel Jo and Kaisa saying things. I can hear Case saying I'm home now. I don't know how many times they say these things, but my body feels like it finally gives out, it's like I become more like liquid, like my bones cease to hold their shape. I just melt into the four of them. I feel and hear my sobs. I feel myself fading into them. I lose consciousness, but I don't think I notice.

REEVES

I may have finally found some competition in the bear hug department.

It's hard to believe that I've been living in Chicago for a couple months now. It's hard to believe that just last week no one was sure what would happen with Mercury. It's hard to believe I felt the swell of joy I did seeing Mercury wrapped around Ella in the bed this morning. It's hard to believe that August is almost here. I always like that month, not like Ella who swears it is her month, but a lot. It always feels like the beginning of something to me, maybe something beautiful. It's hard to believe so many things are hard to believe. Most of all, it's hard to believe that when Mercury hugged me on the porch just now, I realized that they might be just as big of a hugger as I am now that they're opening up in our family.

I felt the strength in their arms, and for a second there, despite the vast difference between their body and mine, I thought they were going to pick me up like I know they do with Ella sometimes. Linsk was working the grill. They were making a combination of grilled vegetables to share with me and Mercury. Mercury, it turns out now that they talk about themselves more, is also a lover of the grill. Linsk appreciates this greatly as one of their favorite things to do is create random grilled medleys for the family to try out. Ella was sitting on the other side of the porch. Her lap looked almost lonely when Mercury got off of it to come hug me. She was reading a book about southern *Girls in Trucks* that she found far more interest in than I could understand on any level. I watched her eyes moving across the page. I looked down at Mercury who was beaming up at me as if they had some magical secret that could light up the night. I grinned far bigger than usual thinking about just how nice it was to see that look, the one that imagines possibilities of an endless variety, on their face the same way I enjoy seeing it come from Linsk, Ella, and other members of the family.

I couldn't help it. I began to cry a little bit. My chest heaved. My eyes watered. I saw Linsk smiling as they came to me. They patted my chest, pulled my lips to theirs, and laughed as Ella informed Mercury that the juice for my juicy muscles might actually come from the powerful tear ducts I kept hidden from most of the world. Mercury's smile launched into the night like a signal flare for the stars to follow on their way home. The combined smell of the vegetables mingling with the wine and the late July breeze only made me cry even more. I watched as Case and Kaisa came up the back steps onto the deck. They both hugged Mercury, and it almost looked like Mercury was going to match me tear for tear. Maybe, I thought, I have competition in the waterworks department as well.

MICHELLE

I feel like something changed inside me after Case told me what Mercury said.

I had this powerful image of my mother floating in my head. That is not unusual at all. I thought about my mom every day, often many, many times each day. I could focus the image and see her in a billowing blouse smiling at the sunset on the back porch of my childhood home. I still missed her every time anything good, bad, or even just ordinary happened. It had been years since I almost called her as a result of some news, but I still felt the urge, and on some level, I hoped I always would. I remembered how we told each other everything when I was just a small girl. I remembered how she would encourage me to chase my dreams and only accept the best life or people had to offer. I thought about these things as tears came running down my face while Case spoke. Something inside me, maybe the piece of my mother that drives me each day, told me to call Mercury that night. I picked up the phone with one thing certain in my mind, this young person would never be left alone again.

We met for coffee at Same Day Café the next afternoon. Mercury was amazed that Ella had stayed over at their, as they called it, shitty apartment for four days straight after that night at Case and Kaisa's house. They were shocked that no one hated them. They were shocked that no one was leaving them. They were shocked that Linsk and Reeves came by bringing coloring books, smiles, and hugs. They were shocked that I was taking them out to coffee. I told them about my mom. It's not a subject I talk about a lot. I told them how I had the opposite experience of their own, that I never had to imagine what it would be like without someone always by my side until I was an adult. I told them that I wanted them to know that no matter what happened, no matter what time, I would be there. I would stand with them like the family did for all of us, but even more so, like their own parents should have. I was not surprised when they started crying. I was not surprised when I hugged them. I was not surprised that the thank you that came from their lips was fairly close to silent. I was only surprised that hugging them felt like the most perfect and right thing in the world.

ANDREI

"It's not that I don't like Taylor Swift," I said as Mercury laughed, "It's that buying those albums in broad daylight from people who know me from the clubs, well, that gave all the guys at the clubs something to give me hell about."

Mercury was sipping on a cider. Ella was over on the other side of the bar laughing with some people who recognized her from the back cover of one of her books. Michelle was at the bar getting both of us drinks with Jo. I was trying to think of something witty to say when I sat down in front of Mercury, but they beat me to the punch when they asked about my embarrassment buying Taylor Swift albums on vinyl for them. Damn Ella, I should have known she would have fun with this, and that Mercury, once they began to open up, would have the same kind of biting, smartass wit it seemed like Ella always surrounded herself with. As if it wasn't hard enough to keep up with the witty remarks that seemed to fall like rain in a hurricane from Michelle and Linsk, I smiled noticing a similar kind of sense of humor starting to show up and pop out from Mercury as July came to a close. Michelle slid into the booth across from me wrapping her arms around Mercury. The two of them had plans to go up to Northwestern and meet up with some of the people Mercury would be working with in the Fall. They were doing this in the morning. I was just out having drinks for the hell of it. I had a gig later in the night, but I was ready for it.

I took a sip of the drink Michelle placed in front of me before sitting in the booth. There was something about the growing relationship between the two of them that made me feel especially calm. Michelle was always looking for someone to help. Her and Linsk and Kaisa would help everyone in the world if given the resources and the chance. I got the feeling that Mercury shared this passion for saving the world with them. I didn't understand it, personally, like Ella I kind of just wanted to live each day, relax with my art, and take care of these would-be world savers as best I could. But I don't know, there was just something about seeing Mercury and Michelle going over the details of the plans Michelle and Linsk were working on that just felt, well, right. I just sat there sipping my drink and enjoying the conversation. I had a feeling that Linsk was right, Mercury would join them and Michelle and Kaisa in their efforts to save the world in every possible way they could come up with in the years to come.

Ella arrived at the table a few minutes later with Linsk and Case. The three of them were grinning about something, but I didn't know what. Linsk was grinning the way they do when some project goes especially well or helps someone even more than they hoped. After a few minutes, Linsk took advantage of a break in the conversation between Michelle and Mercury to tell us all we just had to come outside. We followed because, well, that's what you do when Linsk says to do something. There really isn't any question about it at this point. Anytime our family needs or wants a leader, all eyes turn to Linsk and it seems like they just understand and embrace this role in our lives. Outside, Reeves was standing on the sidewalk holding a really nice set of Levenger. I can't pretend they were really his usual style, he was more the flannel shirt type honestly, but there was a certain beauty to the image as we all found our way to the space on the sidewalk in front of him. "So," Linsk said smiling, "Someone is starting their graduate education in the next couple weeks, and we thought it was fitting that this someone should have some nice bags to carry all their important papers."

There were tears welling in Mercury's eyes as everyone around them smiled. Michelle had passed on a conversation where Mercury talked about how much they loved fancy journals, or methodological notebooks as Michelle would say, the other day over dinner to Ella, Linsk, and Reeves. Mercury had told Michelle that one day they would have a great job, and when they did, they would have fancy bags to match their journals. Linsk decided there was no reason our newest family member should have to wait. With Reeves along for the ride, they went out and found some that, as they said in the midst of Mercury's tears on the sidewalk, "Just kind of feels like it belongs with you little crow."

JO

"It's going to be great, you're going to be amazing, just trust me," I told Twitter Boy on the phone when he called from the airport.

He was nervous about the trip. He was scared he would not fit in well with the family. He was over-thinking things in the ways we both do, like, all the time. He was going on and on and on about forgetting this or that detail about some member of the family in a particularly important moment. It was adorable. He was losing it. He was, though he didn't seem to understand it, demonstrating exactly why he had nothing to worry about. He was coming to meet the people I loved the most, the kind of people that would see how nervous he is and know that he loved me too, that I was important, that I was worth worrying about like that. He was getting on his plane. He was getting off the phone. He was saying he loved me for the nineteenth time since we got on the phone, he repeats the phrase when he's nervous and doesn't know what to say. He was going to do great, but I guess he would have to find out for himself.

"Open up, open up, open up," I heard coming from outside the door to my apartment. The words were followed by a knock too timid to accompany the words. It was the way I arrived at people's houses. It made me smile to hear the phrase from Mercury.

I answered the door. They were standing there carrying a Levenger bag, probably the one Linsk picked out for them, and smiling. They were blushing. "I thought you were supposed to be meeting Ella at Washington Square Park?" Ella always went for a walk in the park when she started a new story, well, started here meaning got past the first three chapters. She had decided that, this time, the park in question would be Washington Square Park. I don't know why she picked that one, but I figured it was as good as any and she did like to make fun of my trips to dream about the cars at the dealerships down the road from the park, so maybe that was it. With Ella, it was as likely an explanation as anything else.

"I'm on my way," Mercury said, "But I needed to tell you something that I should have said a long time ago."

"Oh, goody, what is it love?"

"I love you, Jo," they said smiling with tears in their eyes, "I don't just appreciate you. I love you and you mean so much to me that I don't even know how to understand it."

I wrapped my arms around them. I felt their tears on my shoulder and my own falling down my face. "You do know I always knew that, right, I knew what you were saying when you told me you appreciated me?"

I feel them nod against my chest, and then, looking up into my eyes, they say, "But now that I can," they smiled bigger, "I really wanted to say the words."

KAISA

There was something different about the sunset on the first of August.

I don't mean that there was actually something different about the sunset itself. I mean it felt different. I'm not sure if that was clear. I was standing on the back porch. I was watching the clouds and the sun do the dance they are so well known for throughout the world. I was thinking about Twitter Boy arriving in town soon. I was thinking about Reeves appearing to become more and more comfortable. I was thinking about Mercury asleep in the other room with two of the cats. I was thinking about Case on the couch where they fell asleep right after finishing *The Shining* on DVD, and right after spending the entire movie complaining about how terrible it was compared to the book. Michelle left after Case fell asleep. Mercury didn't make it to the halfway point of the film. Ella and Jo missed movie night. They were up north on Devon because there was a restaurant nearby and a store Ella liked. Ella wanted to use the spaces in the new novel. There was some event there tonight. I wondered if they would come by on their way back.

The sun almost seemed to whisper through the sky. I took a sip of my tea. My back had been troubling me for a few days, but standing felt okay, finally, again. I stared at the porches that sat on the backs of other apartments. The sunset felt different. Sunsets usually signify the end of the day, but something about this one felt like a new day. Linsk had been here for over a year. Ella and Reeves followed as I knew they would. Case and all the others made plans to stay here long term. I smiled. This is home. This is where my family is, where I belong. I wondered how Twitter Boy's visit would go. I knew that Jo was in love with him. The family was looking forward to the visit, but I was pretty sure he was terrified. I thought about Mercury's last few weeks. I wondered what they would have said if I would have found them before New Year's and told them this would be their life. I wondered, not for the first time, what younger me would have said if I could find them in the Village and tell them what was coming, what was waiting for them, what was good enough to hold on with all their might for all those dark years.

CASE

"We're going to be late, you know that right," I ask Ella as she comes out of the apartment on the fourth floor of the building across the street from Dave and Buster's on North Clark Street.

"And if we're late, then what," Ella says giggling and pulling on her auburn hair as we move down the stairs. The landlord let her tour the apartment. She says her character lives there. She says she feels like there are beautiful stories waiting to happen in the place. She says she feels like someone far more special than words lived there once upon a time. She gets these feelings when she is writing, I don't even question it anymore. "The world will explode? Linsk will hate you? No, everyone will hate you? Elephants wearing purple that so does not match like anything will dance across the stage and disrupt your dissertation defense? What exactly does anxiety brain tell you will happen if we are just a smidge late to the party?"

"You're an asshole, you know that," I say laughing at an unfortunately accurate depiction of the way my mind works.

"And that's one of the many reasons you love me."

"Did you find out anything good about your character?"

"Nothing I would share with the likes of you," Ella says shaking her head and turning toward the red line. "Come on Case, we're going to be late," she says sticking her tongue out at me. We head for the red line and I just kind of want to punch and hug her all at the same time. Maybe I'll do a painting of that exact scene, you know, visualize what it's like to bounce around the city with Ella when her writer side is taking over and nothing but sarcasm and random adventures to various places can keep her occupied for more than a few minutes. "But no, I think I got good stuff, I just have a good feeling about that place, seems like the kind of apartment where people who really love each other would read in bed together."

"I'm not even sure what that means."

"I'm not either, but it feels good, special, the way a fond memory can warm you in the middle of a snowstorm," she says as we hop off the train on State Street. Twitter Boy has arrived, we were informed by Jo, and Linsk's welcome party or excuse to have food and laughs in Millennium Park with the family is supposed to be starting right now. Ella takes off in the usual direction, the way she has to go to the park, the way that takes us past that little storefront window part of Pizano's. I catch up to her and wrap my arm around her waist. She smiles at me and pecks me on the top of my head. She pulls me close with her own arm wrapping around my waist. I smile back at her and nuzzle my head against her neck. We move down the sidewalk in silence. Without either of us needing to say anything, we stop in front of Pizano's, light our respective types of Camel cigarettes, and stand together arm-in-arm.

"What are you thinking," I ask her as she turns to look in the window at a small child fighting with a gigantic slice of pizza.

"If I'm being completely honest with you," she says smiling, "I'm trying to see myself, who I used to be, on the other side of this window."

"What would you tell her?"

Laughing, Ella says, "Hey kid, no one told you this, but you can love even more than you are hurting right now."

LINSK

"No, Mercury, you are not doing that, you just can't do that," I said trying not to laugh nearly as hard as I was in the middle of the park.

"What," Mercury said matching my laughter, "You said it yourself, we need to make Twitter Boy feel welcome because it can be intimidating meeting all of us at the same time, I'm just trying to do my part, I mean," and here I see the twinkle in their eye and I can't help but pull them close to me, "What could be better than us only speaking to him in 280 character statements at a time, maybe it will make him feel right at home?"

"Don't you even start, we've already got to manage Ella potentially disappearing at any moment because a particularly interesting squirrel runs by her." Laughing even louder than I was because they had already seen Ella randomly disappear when an idea struck her in the midst of this newest writing phase, Mercury pulls me in even closer and smiles. We stand there watching Andrei and Reeves as they set up chairs for everyone to use. There is a concert in the park tonight, and Michelle went to see who was playing. Jo said her and Twitter Boy were only a couple blocks away when she texted me a few minutes ago. Case said Ella was obsessed with some apartment north of the loop, and they would be here as soon as possible. I point to the place where I put down the containers full of food and other supplies. Mercury trots or hops or walks, sometimes it's hard to tell, over to the containers and begins digging in them.

I stare at the sky for a minute. My family will all be here tonight. There is something about that, about even having a family, that seems so strange. It is Ella's month as she will remind us all each day until September 1st. Mercury starts school in a couple weeks. Reeves has his first gallery opening at the end of the month. I see Kaisa arrive smiling with the quarter-sized spots of blush on their face that never seem to leave no matter their mood or whatever might be happening. I feel warm all over despite a chill in my bones throughout the day. My autoimmune condition is under control, and I've been able to enjoy the summer more than I expected. There are some new steroids and enzymes that seem to be doing the trick. Kaisa wraps their arms around me in a hug that says more than any group of words we could share. I smile and pat the back of the flannel shirt they are wearing tonight. I watch as they move across the grass saying hello to each of the others in whichever way feels best for each encounter.

Chicago, I think, feels right. It feels like home already. It feels like the family was a kind of caterpillar that is blossoming into a butterfly now that we all get to be together in person more often and now that Ella and Jo are bringing in new members to join us in our new home. It's like a turtle or a snail coming out of their shells to hug the sunlight, a family bursting forth from the shadows, ghosts, and pains different, but similar enough, pasts into a bright new morning. From where I stand, I can just make out two shapes that I am sure are Case and Ella. There is something about Ella's form that I can pick out from any distance these days. Maybe that's part of someone really becoming a piece of you, or whatever folks who write about such things call the connections that become too deep for words. I know what they're doing. I understand it. I know they'll join the rest of us in just a few minutes. I wonder just how much rambling about the apartment Ella will do throughout the night, but as the thought crosses my mind, I see Jo and, based on photos, Twitter Boy coming toward me. He looks just about scared enough to be good enough for Jo, and I smile as he extends his hand for me to shake.

ELLA

"What are you thinking about," Mercury asks as we walk through the loop.

I can still taste Linsk's perfect lips on mine. I can still hear Case laughing as Twitter Boy did an impression of Jo. I can still see the red on Jo's cheeks during the impression. I can still feel the smile that spread across my face as Reeves wrapped Linsk in his arms, and the two of them headed for Logan Square. I can still feel the weight of Kaisa's hand on my shoulder as we stood beside Michigan Avenue because, of course, Case forgot something as we were leaving. I can still feel the hug Michelle wrapped around Mercury and I as her, Andrei, Kaisa, and Case headed for the red line that Mercury and I will be taking after I get coffee at the Dunkin Donuts on Adams Street, like I always do when I'm in the loop at night. I can hear Andrei laughing as the four of them disappeared underground as Mercury kissed me softly on the sidewalk.

"I was thinking about how it feels like a new life, here in Chicago, just like it felt when I found Case and Linsk in Miami all those years ago, I don't know, I guess I was thinking about how beautiful, how lucky I guess, I feel to keep getting to begin again, to start wonderful new chapters in my life." Mercury smiles up at me. I cup their chin in my fingers. I kiss them, careful not to spill my coffee or knock their chocolate chip muffin on the sidewalk the way I did a few weeks ago at a different Dunkin' in a different part of the city. "I was thinking about how I can feel Linsk no matter where I am or where they go. I was thinking about how I crave the look in Case's eyes when they just finished a good book. I don't know, I was just thinking about the family, I guess, and how grateful I am for all of y'all." I run my finger down, then up, Mercury's cheek the way that seems to automatically soften their expression.

"I'm starting to agree with Case," Mercury whispers in my ear after pulling my head close to their own, "There is a bit of an emo poet inside you, maybe not as good a poet as Linsk," they giggle because we all know damn near nothing compares to Linsk's poetic talent, "But a poet that, I'm guessing, shares some of the space in your head with the novelist." I squirm the way I do when they whisper in my ear. They take my hand. We walk toward the red line together. My hand in theirs, our steps in sync with one another as if we were following a cadence for a planned march, I stop on the sidewalk after we turn onto State Street. I pull back from them and raise my hand. They giggle the way they did the first time I did this. Without a word, they twirl around in a circle and land in my arms with a kiss on the bridge of my nose.

"It's a dangerous thing," I say as they move back from my face smiling, "Agreeing with Case about anything, that is," at which point they punch me softly in the arm. It reminds me of the ways Linsk punches me, short rapid-fire motions extending their long, slender arms as if in beat to a song, playfully when we're dancing around the kitchen. It reminds me of the ways Case just smacks my shoulder playfully when I feel like the emotions are too real and I start making jokes about us taking a break or not talking for a while. It's not the same. The movements are different. The feeling of Mercury's hand is different. It's not the same, but there is something similar there, something each of these gestures has in common, something that makes my heart swim and allows the me that sat alone in a window years ago to rest in peace.

MERCURY

I'll never forget the moment I embraced Ella and her, no, our family.

She was on the bed. She was on her stomach. She was kicking her feet in her sleep the way she did sometimes for reasons unknown even to her or Linsk. Her head was on my stomach. I was watching her sleep. I could feel her breathing. I was somehow sure I could feel her heartbeat. I watched the strands of her auburn hair flanking the smooth, brown skin of her back. I felt safer in my own bed than I would have once thought possible. I realized the darkness outside was not necessarily problematic for me. I was stroking her hair. I remembered brushing it on the first of August, her month she would say, just two nights before in this same spot. I was thinking about Linsk saying Ella somehow found or generated glitter. I was staring at the random piece of glitter she somehow got in the tiny arch at the beginning of her lower back. I was wondering where she found glitter. I could hear Linsk answer, everywhere.

The opening chords of Taylor Swift's "Begin Again" began to fill my ears from the record player against the wall between the windows across from our bed. I remember smiling at the first time I thought of it as one of our beds. I knew this was the last song on the last side of the album. I thought about starting it again when the record finished. I didn't want to move. I listened to the song and thought about the unexpected 2018 I was having so far. I felt Ella squirm in her sleep. I rubbed her cheek the way she sometimes touches mine. I remembered Ella picked the record right when we got back from the party in the park where we met Twitter Boy. I remember Ella wanted to hear "Red" because she loves that song. I remembered the warmth in my body, in my bones, as we said goodbye to Linsk and the others at the park, in the loop, and only for a small piece of time before we would be together again.

The record finished playing. My phone told me what time it was, 11:45 p.m. I thought again, for a second, about getting up to restart it or put on another album. We had danced while the record played. Ella wanted to cuddle. I did too, but she said it first tonight. I thought about a group hug between the two of us and Linsk and Reeves in the middle of the park. My family, I thought, our family. I felt a smile spread across my face. Ella and Linsk always seem to glow when they're near each other. I feel like we do it too around them – Reeves, the others, and maybe even me. I didn't realize forty-five minutes had passed in silence until I checked my phone. I tried to remember the last time silence didn't feel suffocating. I couldn't. I tried to remember the last time I was awake, alone in the night, without some noise or my phone distracting me from the thoughts in my head. I couldn't. I was surprised that silence could become safe again. I was surprised I didn't want a distraction.

I smiled at the record player and felt Ella shift again in her sleep. I realized that I didn't really need anything, but I wanted so much. I wanted to keep running my hands through Ella's hair. I wanted to spend as many nights with her as I could. I wanted to get used to feeling safe and comfortable in silence, in darkness, and well, in a family. I wanted to grow closer to Linsk, Reeves, Case, Kaisa, Jo, Andrei, Michelle, and even Twitter Boy as long as he treated Jo well. I wanted to embrace the people I love who, somehow, I now know, love me too. I wanted to soak in this moment with Ella, the joy of the time we all spent in the park earlier, and the feeling that there finally was a place where I truly belong. I guess I just wanted to let it all wash over me in a warm, comforting bath since via Chicago I found a family.

SUGGESTED CLASS ROOM OR BOOK CLUB USE

DISCUSSION AND HOME WORK QUESTIONS

1. *Via Chicago* explores the ways families form over time, and what it means to be a family. What are some ways you come to consider certain people family, and how did your own family form?
2. Throughout the novel, multiple narrators recount the same moments, but notice different things in each moment. What do you think other people might notice that you do not in any given situation or interaction? How might you learn such information?
3. *Via Chicago* focuses on a group of people who become family while bonding over and healing from past trauma. What are some ways they manage negative events, and how do these types of events bond people?
4. The characters in the novel form and maintain varied types of relationships throughout the book. Think of your own life and relationships, how do the experiences of the characters compare?
5. The novel explores some ways gender and sexualities may shape the experiences of people in society. What are some ways, positive and / or negative, gender and sexualities may shape your own life, relationships, and experiences?

CREATIVE WRITING ASSIGNMENTS

1. Pick one of the characters in the novel and move forward in time ten years. What is their life like, where do they live, and what do they do for a living? Compose a story that answers these questions.
2. Re-write the first chapter of the novel from the perspective of another person who is not a narrator in this story.
3. Pick a character in the story, and write their experience coming home after the cookout at the end of the story.
4. Beginning after the final chapter of the novel, continue Mercury's narration, what happens to them next?

5. Pick a scene that the characters talk about in the book (i.e., some event you learn about in conversation, but do not witness with the narrators), and write that scene from the perspective of any character.

QUALITATIVE RESEARCH ACTIVITIES

1. Select any conversation or event in the book and conduct a focus group to learn how other people interpret that conversation or event.
2. Select a character and do a content analysis of that character. How do they talk? How do they see the world? What are their relationships (romantic, friendship, family, or otherwise) like? In what ways are they similar or different in relation to other characters? What information about them is missing and what information is presented in the novel? Overall, what can we learn from that character?

ABOUT THE AUTHOR

J. E. Sumerau is the author of six novels – *Cigarettes & Wine, Essence, Homecoming Queens, That Year, Other People's Oysters* (with Alexandra C. H. Nowakowski), and *Palmetto Rose* – as well as over 80 scholarly works concerning the intersections of sexualities, gender, health, religion, and violence in society. She is also an associate professor and the director of applied sociology at the University of Tampa as well as the co-founder and primary editor of www.writewhereithurts. net. For more information, please visit www.jsumerau.com or follow her on Twitter @jsumerau.

Printed in the United States
By Bookmasters